Candle Making Business

How to Launch a Thriving Six-Figure Candle Business from Home

Alyssa Garner and Garrett Garner

Disclaimer

Note from the authors: Below is the standard disclaimer that books like this typically include. To summarize in our own words, we would like you to know that starting or running a business of any kind comes with inherent risk. If you choose to take the leap, you alone are responsible for the actions and choices you make in your business. While we wish you all the success in the world, we can't make any guarantees that the steps outlined here will have any particular outcome for you, as results are based on many factors. Always consider your decisions carefully, while also maintaining a healthy dose of optimism!

The information in this book is for informational and educational purposes only. It should not be construed as business, tax, or legal advice of any kind. All information and resources found in this book are based on the opinions of the authors alone unless otherwise noted.

The authors of this book assume no responsibility or liability for any consequence resulting directly or indirectly from any action or inaction you take based on the information found in this book.

While the authors have made every effort to provide accurate information at the time of publication, they do not assume any responsibility for errors or changes that occur after publication.

This book is intended to be used only as a general guide, and not as a sole source of information on the subject matter. Always consult a licensed professional before attempting any techniques outlined in this book.

Congrats!

Congratulations on picking up this book! You currently hold in your hands the keys to successfully launching your very own candle making business.

We're SO excited to hear what you think! Once you've finished the book, we would love it if you'd leave an honest review on Amazon.

Your review provides valuable feedback and helps us bring more books and resources to you. We appreciate your support!

Contents

Introduction

Have you dreamed of running your own six-figure business, but don't know where to start? You've come to the right place!

With this book, you won't just be starting a thriving business from scratch. You'll be successfully launching one of the EASIEST and most PROFITABLE businesses for beginners: a candle making business!

Even if you've never made a candle before, you can start a successful candle business in as little as 30 days using the step-by-step framework in this book.

We've provided you with a blueprint for surefire success that is practical, reproducible, and, most importantly, easy to follow. If you stick to it and put in the work, in just a few months, your bank account (and life) could look drastically different.

The Why

So, let's begin with the basics: why candles? The simple answer is because people LOVE them.

The candle market is booming and growing every year. Even in a recession or a pandemic, there is always high demand for candles. In fact, the candle making industry is expected to reach nearly $5 billion by 2026 in the US alone.

So, what does that mean for you? Get in now, when there's still plenty of room to stand out and make your mark. With the candle industry booming, there's never been a better time to start your business than right now.

Besides that, candles are fun! There are so many different types, scents, and styles that you can play with. You can put your own unique spin on a basic candle and create an exciting brand that your customers will love.

Whether they're used for home decor, yoga, aromatherapy, or just for fun, candles are here to stay and you can be part of a lasting industry that creates beauty and promotes relaxation for its customers.

Also, candles have a low barrier to entry. You can make them at home and sell them online. There are even little-known ways to create passive income from candles on autopilot (we'll show you how later on!).

It's cheap and easy to get started—you just need some basic supplies. According to candlescience.com, the average cost of manufacturing a candle is $3.78 and the candle can then be sold for three to four times its cost.

That's a HUGE profit margin. To give you an idea of how amazing this is, the average markup (the amount added to an item's price that reflects profit) for a retail product is only around 30%–60%. With candles, it's 200%–300%. That alone is a compelling enough reason to start a candle business over any other.

Finally, anyone can learn to make a candle using a basic recipe and then experiment from there to grow their inventory. Candles are easy to customize simply by changing scents or colors. It's easy for newbies to get started, yet the options for growth and expansion are endless.

Whether you love candles or your goal is simply to start a sustainable business that makes money in any economy, a candle making business is a smart way to scale your income quickly.

The How

Before we dive in, here's a quick overview of how this book works. We recommend reading through the entire book FIRST before taking action, so you can understand how the different components work together.

First, we'll start with the basics of candle making. We'll tell you exactly what you'll need, where to buy it, and provide a simple step-by-step recipe, so you can make your first candle right away.

When it comes to launching a business, one of the biggest obstacles is simply getting started. That's why we'll provide you with an easy approach to making candles, so you can get your business off the ground quickly. Once you've made your first few candles, you'll be hooked!

After that, we'll provide helpful guidance for customizing your candles, so you can grow your inventory and provide your customers with different options. We'll go over the various types of candles, waxes, colors, vessels, and more, so you can experiment for yourself and create unique products that reflect who you are.

While this step is exciting, don't get too caught up in customization yet. Remember, our goal is to get you into business and making money as quickly as possible. Focus on making the basic candle first and save customization for later.

Your thriving business starts with just that one basic candle in a few different scents. Once you have that, you're ready to start selling. It's that easy!

After this, we'll dive into the business side of things. We'll start by teaching you the essential business principles that will ensure your candle making business is set up for success and profit from the very beginning.

Next, you'll learn how to brand, package, price, and market your candles. We'll share the best platforms for selling and our proven strategies for making sales quickly and consistently.

You'll also learn how to make your business official with an LLC alongside easy tips for staying on top of taxes, accounting, and insurance. Don't worry—we'll keep this section nontechnical and easy to understand, so you can stay on top of your business with ease.

Finally, we'll share powerful strategies for scaling and automating your candle making empire. You'll learn how to grow your business, so it increases in revenue each year, while simultaneously reducing your workload.

We'll even teach you how to create passive income with your candle business, so you can make money while you sleep, vacation, and spend time with family (this chapter alone is a total game changer!).

Are you feeling excited? Let's do it!

CHAPTER 1

Let's Make a Candle

Now that you understand the why and the how, let's make your first candle!

If you've never made a candle before, the hardest part is simply getting started, which is why this chapter will be super easy and straightforward.

In the next chapter, we'll go through the different types of candles, waxes, wicks, fragrances, colors, and more. This will allow you to customize your candles and make them your own later on.

But for now, our goal is to provide the simple step-by-step way to create your first batch of candles, so you can see how fun and easy it is!

This will also allow you to start selling your candles right away, so you can make money first, and customize later. By following the instructions in this chapter, you can have your first lot of inventory ready to go within a week!

Once you start making and selling candles, you'll be hooked and eager to progress from there.

So let's start with the basics. Container candles are the most popular type of candle and the easiest for beginners to make, so that's what you'll learn here.

A container candle is basically just like it sounds. It's a candle that comes in its own nonflammable container, such as a tin or glass jar.

You don't need to worry about dye or any other fancy elements because the container itself is the decorative element. This makes it even easier for a beginner to start with.

You'll make this first candle out of paraffin wax. It's easy to work with and can hold a high amount of fragrance.

Then, you'll use fragrance oil, which is specifically formulated for candles, soaps, and similar products, to add a unique scent to your candle. These oils come in a large variety of scents and are precisely engineered to create a long-lasting aroma.

We recommend starting with paraffin wax and fragrance oil since they're inexpensive and ideal for beginners. However, if you'd prefer a natural and eco-friendly alternative, at the end of this chapter, we'll show you how to modify the basic recipe, so you're using soy wax and essential oil instead.

If you're already skilled at making candles, feel free to skim the next two chapters or simply skip to chapter 3 to start setting up your business!

One final tip before we get started: Be sure to read this chapter in FULL before you start making your candles. It contains important safety and troubleshooting tips you'll want to be aware of before getting started.

Materials

Here's what you'll need to make two 12-ounce container candles:

1 pound of paraffin wax – we recommend IGI 4630 paraffin wax, which is ideal for container candles and comes in slab form; you can order a 10-pound slab from candlescience.com or, if you want to start smaller, you can get just 2 pounds from theflamingcandle.com.

2 pre-tabbed and pre-waxed 6" wicks – we like the LX 14 6" wick from candlescience.com or the EricX Light 6" wick, which you can find on Amazon.

1 ounce of fragrance oil of your choice – you can search under "fragrance oils" on candlescience.com or theflamingcandle.com to find a scent that sounds exciting to you (they have every scent imaginable from lavender chamomile to pumpkin peanut brittle); note that fragrance oils are NOT the same as essential oils (essential oils are challenging for beginners because they're volatile and evaporate more quickly—we'll explore essential oils later on).

2 (12-ounce) nonflammable containers with lids – you can find these on candlescience.com or you can search on Amazon; feel free to use any jar or container you'd like as long as it's nonflammable and 12 ounces (hint: mason jars are a great place to start!).

2 wick stickers – these are used to secure your wick to the bottom of the container; we recommend the large wick stickers or the wick stickers pro from candlescience.com; alternatively you can use a bit of melted wax or glue to adhere your wick to the container.

Labels – every candle needs a warning label and a brand label; you won't need these until after the candle is made, so we'll discuss them in detail later on.

Equipment

Here's the necessary equipment for making your candles:

Knife – for cutting the wax; you can purchase a soap cutter from Amazon or use a long carving knife.

Small measuring cup – for measuring your fragrance oil; a 4-ounce glass cup works the best (some fragrance oils can create holes in plastic cups).

Double boiler – for melting the wax; can be found on Amazon, Target, Bed Bath & Beyond, or anywhere else that sells cookware; make sure the double boiler is large enough to accommodate your pouring pitcher.

Pouring pitcher – for pouring the wax into the containers; we recommend one made from aluminum because it helps the wax cool faster and is easier to clean; the pouring pitcher from candlescience.com, which holds up to 4 pounds of melted wax, is a good choice.

Kitchen scale – for weighing your wax; can be purchased on Amazon or anywhere that kitchen equipment is sold; we recommend one that measures in grams for the most accurate reading.

Stirring utensil – disposable bamboo stirrers, which can be purchased on Amazon or Walmart, work well for this because you can use each stirrer once and then throw it away (which saves cleanup time); alternatively, you can use a silicone spatula or small wooden spoon.

Thermometer – a small glass or digital thermometer works well for this; can be purchased at candlescience.com or any kitchen supply store.

2 wick holders (also called wick bars) – for holding your wicks in place while your candles are cooling; can be found on candlescience.com or Amazon; alternatively, you can use a clothespin to secure the wicks.

Wick trimmer – used to trim down the wick after the candles have cooled; you can also use sharp kitchen scissors but they're less accurate and can fray the wick.

The following is optional equipment for making your candles. While these items aren't strictly necessary, they will make the process easier and ensure that your candles turn out correctly every time.

Rubbing alcohol (optional) – for wiping down the container before pouring the wax; this helps the wick sticker adhere completely to the bottom; can also be used for cleanup.

Cotton swab (optional) – for applying the rubbing alcohol to the container.

Rubber gloves (optional, but highly recommended) – protects your hands; nitrile gloves are the best because they are heat-resistant and protect your hands from colorant and fragrance spills (plus they're stronger than latex or vinyl).

Heat gun (optional) – can be used to fix holes or lumps on your candles' surface; ensures each candle you make can be sold (we'll discuss this more in the troubleshooting section).

The Process

1. Use a carving knife or soap cutter to break down the slab of wax into smaller pieces. Weigh 1 pound of wax on your scale and add it to your pouring pitcher.

2. Fill the bottom pot of the double boiler with 1–2 inches of water and place it over low to medium heat.

3. Once the water is boiling, put the pouring pitcher of wax directly inside the top pot (the double boiler insert) and sit it inside the bottom pot.

4. Lower the heat and bring the water in the bottom pot to a gentle simmer. As the water evaporates, you can add more to keep the water level consistent (just make sure the water doesn't splash into the pouring pitcher).

5. Melt the wax to 185 degrees Fahrenheit. Monitor the temperature using the thermometer.

6. While the wax is melting, prepare your containers. Clean each container with an alcohol-soaked cotton swab (if using) then clean off the excess with a paper towel.

7. Put the wick sticker on the bottom of the wick and secure it to the center of the first container. It helps to stand above the candle and look down at it, in order to place the wick as close to the center as possible. You can also use a pen or chopstick to push down on the wick and secure it to your container. Repeat with the second container.

8. Pull the wicks tight and fasten with wick holders.

9. Measure out 1 ounce of fragrance oil using the small measuring cup.

10. Once the wax reaches 185 degrees, add fragrance oil and remove from the heat.

11. Stir wax gently with the stirring utensil for about 30 seconds and allow it to cool to a pouring temperature of 170 degrees Fahrenheit.

12. Pour the wax into your containers and allow to cool overnight at room temperature (a room between 70–77 degrees Fahrenheit is ideal).

13. Once the candles have cooled completely, trim the wick to 1/4 of an inch and secure your lid on top.

14. Let the candles sit for 3–5 more days at room temperature (this is a process called "curing") in order to enhance the scent.

Congrats, you've just made your first candle! See how easy it is?

It can take a bit of time to get into the flow of it, but with a little bit of practice and patience, candle making will soon become a fun (and profitable) activity for you.

Be sure to read on for important safety and troubleshooting tips!

Safety First

Candle making involves handling hot equipment and, oftentimes, working with chemicals. Just like science class, there are guidelines that can (and should) be followed to keep the process fun and safe.

As when cooking in your kitchen, you should have basic fire safety equipment nearby, such as a fire extinguisher and/or fire blanket. You should also have a first aid kit on hand.

Practice common sense when working with hot wax, such as using pot holders when handling hot equipment. You might also want to wear safety goggles when pouring hot wax to protect your eyes.

Wear an apron to protect your clothes and rubber gloves to protect your hands. We recommend nitrile gloves because they're strong and heat-resistant.

Ensure the room you're using for candle making is spacious, well lit, and ventilated. Keep the room tidy and never leave your workspace unattended while you're in the process of making candles. Small children and pets should be kept away from the area as well.

You also want the room to be climate-controlled. Setting the room to the same temperature each time will ensure your candles turn out perfectly uniform from one day to the next. The best temperature range for candle making is between 70–77 degrees Fahrenheit (72 is typically ideal).

If you're making candles in your kitchen, be sure to cover your countertops with newspaper or wax paper to prevent staining or mess. Also make sure to keep anything edible out of your workspace and wipe down all surfaces before preparing food.

If your candle making space is away from your kitchen, you can consider purchasing a portable electric burner. This is also ideal since it keeps your candle making separate from your food preparation.

Finally, you may want to consider wearing a respirator when making candles, especially if you're sensitive to smells or chemicals. We also recommend having an air purifier (we love our Levoit air purifier—we named him "Puffy") to clean the air after you're done working.

If this all sounds like a lot, don't worry. Once you initially set up your space for safety, it basically becomes second nature. Simply follow the basic guidelines and use common sense for a safe and enjoyable candle making experience.

Pro Tips

- Read through all instructions, safety guidelines, and troubleshooting tips before you begin making your first candle. Be sure you have all your materials and equipment ready to go before you get started.

- Our basic candle recipe gives you all the specific ingredients, equipment, and step-by-step processes you'll need to create your first candle with complete ease. The only exception is that we don't recommend a specific fragrance or type of container for your candle because we want you to choose this for yourself. This ensures that your candles will be unique and stand out in the market. After all, we can't have everyone reading this book making the exact same candle, right? We give you all the guidance you need to produce a candle easily with no guesswork, while also giving you a bit of room to make it your own.

- Be sure that you order a single-pour wax. This is easiest for beginners to work with because it doesn't shrink to the point of needing a second pour. If you purchase IGI 4630 paraffin wax, as specified above, you'll only need one pour to complete your candle.

- You may need to experiment with different suppliers to find the ingredients and equipment that work best for you. We recommend candlescience.com, theflamingcandle.com, and lonestarcandlesupply.com. All three are reputable candle making supply companies.

- Always cover your workspace with newspaper or wax paper for easy cleanup.

- The easiest way to clean your equipment after use is to wipe each piece thoroughly with rubbing alcohol and a paper towel. Do this before the wax hardens for the best results.

- After your first candle is finished and cured, you'll want to burn test it before making more. This tests the candle for safety, integrity, and ensures it emits a high-quality burn for your customers. Burn the candle for 3–4 hours at a time and observe it for any issues. Do this several times until the candle burns away completely. See the troubleshooting section for common issues that may come up during the burn test and how the fix them.

Troubleshooting

If your first candle isn't perfect, don't despair! Here are ways to troubleshoot common errors:

Sinkholes

A sinkhole is a round cavity, usually near the wick, that appears when the wax hardens. It occurs when the wax at the edge of the jar and around the wick cools faster than the rest of the candle.

To avoid sinkholes, ensure the correct temperature for both your wax and your workspace. Your container should also be at room temperature or even slightly warm (never cold) when you pour the wax.

To fix a sinkhole, hold a heat gun about six to eight inches over your candle and rotate in a circular motion until the melted wax fills the sinkhole and the top is smooth. Allow the candle to cool and harden before handling it again.

If you don't have a heat gun, you can try the technique above using a hair dryer on the lowest setting. Just be sure not to hold the hair dryer too close or the wax will melt unevenly.

Flickering

When performing a burn test (see pro tips), be on the lookout for wild, unstable, or excessive flickering. This typically means the candle wick is too long. Blow the candle out, let it cool, trim the wick, and try again. If the problem persists, you may need to try a different size or brand of candle wick.

Too Much Soot

If your candle emits a smoky afterburn or is simply releasing too much soot into the container, this also means your wick is too long. Trim it down and try again.

Wick is Off-Center

When making your candle, be sure you pull your wick tight and fasten it securely with your wick holder. This ensures that the wick won't move when the candle is curing.

If you notice your wick is off-center while burning, blow the candle out and re-center it by dipping long tweezers in a 1/2 inch of melted wax and using them to carefully guide the wick back to center.

Wax Pulling Away From Sides

If your candle is pulling away from the sides of your container, this means there's air trapped between the container and the wax. This can be avoided by cleaning the container with rubbing alcohol before pouring the wax.

Not Enough Scent When Lit

If the scent emanating from your lit candle isn't strong enough, you may have added your fragrance at too high or low a temperature. Make sure your wax is 185 degrees Fahrenheit when adding your fragrance oil.

Also make sure you've allowed at least three days for curing, which enhances the scent throw. Generally, the longer you cure your candle, the stronger your scent will be.

No matter what issues you run into, always remember that practice makes progress.

If you're making a candle for the first time, be proud that you tried something new, even if it didn't turn out quite the way you wanted it to. Keep going and don't give up. Over time, candle making will be easy, fun, and even relaxing for you. Just keep at it!

Eco-Friendly Alternative

The basic recipe in this chapter uses paraffin wax and fragrance oil because they're easiest for beginners to start with. That being said, paraffin wax is made from petroleum, which releases chemicals and a higher level of soot. Fragrance oil is easy to measure and very effective at creating a high scent throw, but it's a synthetic substance.

If you'd rather work with natural, eco-friendly ingredients, you can still use the basic recipe from this chapter with a few simple tweaks:

- Soy wax typically comes as flakes instead of a slab. We recommend 1 pound of Golden Brands 464 Soy Wax in place of the IGI 4630.

- You will still heat the wax to 185 degrees Fahrenheit and then add the essential oil. You'll have to experiment to find the right amount for your candle. Start with 50 drops and then increase up to 100 drops until you achieve the optimal scent throw. You can find essential oils on candlescience.com or other candle supply stores.

- The pouring temperature for soy wax is lower than paraffin. You'll want to stir it for two minutes and pour into your containers at 135 degrees Fahrenheit.

- The curing time for soy wax is longer than paraffin. You'll want to cure your candle for 10–14 days for the best scent throw.

- Be aware that soy wax is softer than paraffin wax, which makes it harder to work with. It's also more prone to sinkholes and shrinkage, so make sure to follow those troubleshooting tips to help you along!

- While fragrance oils typically have a set ratio of 1 ounce of fragrance oil to 1 pound of wax, you'll have to play around with essential oils to find the right scent strength for your candle.

While creating your first candle from soy wax and essential oils may be a bit more challenging, it's totally worth it if you're interested in selling natural candles.

Just like with paraffin candles, be patient and keep practicing. Soon enough, you'll be making gorgeous all-natural candles that your customers will love.

Create Your Inventory

Now that you've made your first candle, the next step is to determine how much inventory you'll need in order to launch your business. In this case, inventory is simply how many candles you'll have in stock at one time.

We recommend making 10–15 container candles, based on the instructions above, in three to four different scents to start. This amounts to about 30–60 candles in total. This is a fairly wide range that is largely dependent on the amount of time and materials you have at your disposal.

Since the materials are usually cheaper when purchased in bulk, we suggest buying enough material to make all your candles at once alongside three to four different fragrance oils.

Simply start by making two candles with the same fragrance oil using the directions above. If these turn out well, then make more with the same fragrance until you have 10–15 candles of that scent. After that, repeat the process with your next fragrance oil and then the next until you have 30–60 candles in three to four different scents.

One important thing to be aware of is your supplier's lead times. This is the amount of time that it takes to receive materials from your supplier (e.g., it takes about 1–2 weeks to receive a new shipment of wax from candlescience.com).

If candles in a certain scent are selling faster than others, make sure you're able to restock quickly by knowing how long new materials will take to arrive and how long it will take you to make a new batch.

The goal is to never be out of stock because then you'll be leaving money on the table. Always plan ahead and keep well stocked on all your candles, especially popular ones.

Now that you've learned how to make a basic candle and stock up on inventory, the next chapter will be all about the different ways to customize your candles and make them your own.

CHAPTER 2

Make It Your Own

One of the best things about a candle making business is that it's never boring! There are so many different ways to mix things up and make your candles unique to you and your brand.

You can add mica powder to your candles to make them sparkle. You can mix multiple fragrance oils together to create a brand-new signature scent. You can even use molds to create candles in the shape of cupcakes, flowers, or unicorns. The sky is truly the limit!

In this chapter, we'll explore types of candles, wax, fragrance, wicks, color, vessels, and molds. This will give you the general knowledge needed to expand your candle offerings. At the end of the chapter, we'll teach you best practices and how to get started customizing your candles.

It's important to note that although customizing your candles is exciting, we HIGHLY recommend that you open up your business with just the basic candles to start (see chapter 1). Our goal is to help you open your candle business as quickly and effortlessly as possible, so you can start making money within the first 30 days.

While customizing your candles is really fun, it does take some time, patience, and experimentation. It can be a bit overwhelming for a beginner and you don't need this step in order to make a profit with your business.

Start with the basic candles in chapter 1 first. Focus on setting up shop, branding, and marketing, so you can start selling quickly. Keep practicing the basic recipe until your candles are perfect and making a profit.

Once you've accomplished the above, then come back to this chapter for exciting ways to expand your inventory and bring in new customers.

Types of Candles

Let's start with the different types of candles. In chapter 1, we taught you how to make a basic container candle, but there are lots of other types to explore.

Here are the main types of candles:

Container Candles

This is any candle that comes in its own container, such as a glass jar. The candles you see at Yankee Candle and Bath & Body Works are typically container candles. A tea light can also be considered a container candle.

Votive Candles

These are short, small slow-burning candles that stand on their own. They are typically placed into a holder or votive container for safe burning.

Pillar Candles

A pillar candle is typically made with a hard wax (such as paraffin), so it can stand on its own without a container. They are typically cylindrical with one wick.

Floating Candles

This type of candle is specifically designed to float while it burns. They are placed in a bowl of water, so the light can reflect off the surface and produce a warm glow.

Rolled Candles

These are made by rolling a sheet of wax (usually beeswax) around a wick that's placed in the center.

Taper Candles

These are long, thin candles that are typically unscented. They can't stand on their own and need a holder. They're often displayed on dining tables at fancy restaurants for a romantic touch.

Molded Candles

This is any candle that is made by pouring wax into a form (aka mold) and then removing it once it's set. This type of candle is freestanding and doesn't come in its own container.

Pillar, votive, and floating candles are all molded candles. Novelty candles that are shaped like ice cream cones or teddy bears are also molded candles.

Wax Melts

While not technically a type of candle, wax melts are still a popular item that you can consider selling in your business. They're essentially a candle without a wick.

Wax melts are pieces of scented wax, in various shapes, colors, and sizes. They are placed on top of a warmer and fill the room with fragrance.

Wax

Now, we'll explore the different kinds of wax that can be used for candle making.

Paraffin Wax

This wax is beginner-friendly and easy to work with. It holds a high fragrance load and is very easy to dye. It comes in various melting points, which is helpful when making a variety of candle types. It's also a hard wax that has strength and rigidity, so even tall pillar candles can maintain their shape easily. It's usually the cheapest wax too.

While we recommend paraffin wax for beginners, the main downside is that it's made from petroleum, which is not a renewable resource. Those looking for a cleaner and more natural alternative will want to consider the other waxes on this list.

Soy Wax

This is an eco-friendly alternative to paraffin. It makes beautiful candles that burn slowly and create a pleasant aroma. Soy wax doesn't contain pollutants, creates very little soot, and holds essential oils well.

While it gets major points for being sustainable, soy wax is softer and can be difficult for beginners to work with. It's prone to sinkholes, frosting, and shrinkage. It's also typically more expensive than paraffin wax, but a cheaper alternative to palm, coconut, or beeswax.

Palm Wax

This is a natural wax that offers a clean burn. It's very stable, holds fragrance well, and is great for molded candles (it can be removed from molds easily).

On the flip side, it's generally more expensive than paraffin or soy wax. While palm wax is biodegradable and renewable, it has been unfortunately linked to deforestation issues, as it comes from palm trees.

Coconut Wax

This eco-friendly wax has been growing in popularity over the last few years. It's soft and creamy with a light coconut scent. It also offers a smooth burn and holds scent very well.

Coconut wax typically isn't used on its own in candle making, but rather added to other eco-friendly waxes. In particular, it can be added to soy wax to eliminate wet spots, frosting, and sinkholes (try three parts soy wax to one part coconut wax).

Beeswax

This is considered the healthiest wax, as it is smokeless, sootless, and even purifies the air. On the flip side, it's soft, sticky, and difficult to work with. It's also expensive, but can command a higher price point when sold.

We typically don't recommend this wax, especially for beginners, unless your brand is heavily focused on health and sustainability. If this is the case, you could consider making solely beeswax candles and building your business around that.

Try mixing beeswax with coconut oil, which will lower its melting point and make the beeswax easier to melt and pour. This will also result in a more even burn.

Wax Blends

Many waxes you'll find at candle making supply stores are blends of more than one wax. Blends are often easier to work with because they are mixed and tested for optimal results. You can also experiment with making your own blends, once you've gained more experience in candle making.

At the end of the day, the best type of wax to use depends on your budget, brand, and other priorities, as well as the types of candles you wish to make.

For example, if your top priority is producing candles with minimal cost and maximum ease, paraffin wax is the way to go. However, if you'd rather run an eco-friendly business that's still budget conscious then soy wax is likely a good choice for you. If you want to start a health-based brand and higher start-up costs with a steeper learning curve aren't an issue for you, then you could consider beeswax.

It may take some trial and error, but eventually you'll find the waxes that work best for you. You may also need to experiment with different brands and types of blends as well.

Fragrance

There are two primary ways to add fragrance to your candles: fragrance oils and essential oils.

We recommend fragrance oils to start because they're cheaper and offer more variety. However, essential oils are ideal if you want to make natural candles. Similar to waxes, it all depends on your brand and priorities.

When experimenting with oils, multiply the amount of wax you're using (in ounces) by the percentage of the fragrance or essential oil. This will give you the amount that you should use in ounces.

Wicks

Believe it or not, choosing the right wick is one of the most difficult parts of candle making. Both the size and length of the wick will have a huge impact on your candle.

According to the National Candle Association, there are five major types of wicks:

- **Flat wicks** – knitted wicks that are consistent in their burning and have a self-trimming effect; they are the most commonly used wicks and work great for taper and pillar candles.
- **Square wicks** – knitted wicks that are rounded and a bit stronger than flat wicks; great for beeswax candles and pillar candles.
- **Cored wicks** – knitted wicks with a round cross section that use a core material (such as cotton, zinc, or paper) to keep the wick straight; best for container candles, votive, and pillar candles.
- **Wooden wicks** – wicks that create a soothing crackling sound when burned (such as WoodWick candles by Yankee Candle); great for large container candles if you want to add a crackling fire effect to them.
- **Specialty wicks** – used for specific applications like oil lamps and insect-repelling candles (most candlemakers don't need to worry about this category).

While some wicks work better for certain types of candles, the two most important factors in choosing the right wick are (1) the type of wax and (2) the diameter of the candle.

Most candle making supply stores have a wick guide on their website, so you can easily choose the perfect wick for your candle. Here's the one from candlescience.com, as an example: candlescience.com/learning/wick-guide

Oftentimes, you may need to test out two or three different types of wicks to find the best one for your candle. If your candle doesn't achieve a full melt pool (i.e., the melted wax touches all sides at a rate of about one hour per inch of diameter) or exhibits too much flickering, you should try a different wick.

Color

There are several different ways to add color to your candles. We'll explore each of them here.

As a safety note, when adding dye to your candles, always be sure that the dye is safe to burn (i.e., it has no alcohol in it). It's also generally best to add dye AFTER your fragrance or essential oil, since the oils may change the color of the wax.

Liquid Dye

We suggest using liquid dye when starting out. It's easiest to work with and you can even mix them to create custom colors.

Liquid dyes typically come in a dropper bottle with guidance on which shades the dye will produce in different types of wax. It's easy because you can simply measure out the dye in drops and achieve the perfect shade each time.

Dye Blocks

Dye blocks tend to produce more vibrant colors (especially in soy wax) and are ideal for making large batches of candles. They're usually cheaper since they're bought in bulk.

On the flip side, they're more difficult for beginners because you have to cut and measure the blocks yourself.

Dye Chips

Dye chips are very easy to use and measure out. Like liquid dye, they're great for beginners, but typically more expensive than dye blocks. The biggest challenge is ensuring that the chips dissolve completely, so the color of your candle is even.

Natural Colors

If you want to brand your candles as "all natural," you won't be able to use the artificial dyes listed above. Instead you'll have to experiment with herbs, flowers, and spices. For example, annatto seeds will create a yellow wax, while spirulina will create green.

Please note that using these natural ingredients can be more volatile and we only recommend this for the more experienced chandler.

If selling all-natural candles is a priority for you then we suggest leaving the color out of your candles to start, until you have the time and experience to dabble in natural colors.

Mica

Mica is a naturally occurring mineral that lends a slight shimmer to candles. The issue with mica is that the powder doesn't fully dissolve if you mix it directly into the wax. This can lead to clogging the wick and a smaller flame.

If you want to add mica to your candle, we suggest rubbing it on the surface of a cooled candle, rather than mixing it into the wax. It's also ideal for making wax melts since these contain no wick.

Vessels

Vessel is simply a fancy word for the container that holds your candle. As such, this section is only relevant to candles that come in a container and not freestanding ones.

Vessels are typically made from glass, ceramic, or tin. They can be as simple as a glass mason jar or as intricate as a flowerpot decorated with rhinestones. Just be sure that the vessels you choose are resistant to heat, fire, cracks, and leaks.

It's generally best to choose vessels that are specifically designed for candle making, so you know they're safe. You can browse the many options at candle supply stores, such as candlescience.com.

Choosing a variety of vessels is a super easy way for beginners to start customizing their candles. The exact same candle (wax, wick, and scent) can be made into multiple distinct candles simply by pouring it into different vessels of the same size (in the case of the basic recipe, this will be 12 ounces). This allows you to diversify your inventory without changing up your recipe.

Just choose the same container in three different colors and you suddenly have three unique candles instead of just one. This also allows you to do market research on which one sells the best.

You can similarly expand your inventory by pouring the same candle into vessels of different sizes, shapes, or styles, but you may need to adjust the wax amount and wick size accordingly.

Once you find a few vessels that you like for your candles, it's cheapest to buy them wholesale (in bulk).

Molds

If you're not using a vessel for your candle, you'll need a mold. We recommend silicone molds to start because they're cheap, user-friendly, and easy to clean.

Similar to vessels, there are a large variety of molds to help you customize your candles quickly and easily. The simplest one to start with is a pillar candle mold. It's all one large cylinder, so it's easy to work with and avoids the frustration of smaller pieces breaking off.

Another easy candle mold to start with is a shell-shaped one. You'll be able to make pretty, beachy candles without any hassle at all.

Once you get the hang of pillar or shell molds, you can graduate to more intricate ones. The sky is truly the limit with molds and there are endless possibilities. You can even experiment with making your own molds down the line to create candles that are truly unique.

A quick tip when using molds: For easy removal, use a candle mold release spray before pouring the wax. Alternatively, you could try a very light spray of canola oil, but be aware that this could create a sticky film on the finished candle. If you still have trouble removing the candle, put the mold in the freezer for 5–10 minutes.

How to Customize Your Candles

So now that you're an expert in all things candles, the next question is how to use this information to customize your products.

Here are the basic ways to customize your candles:

- Container or mold
- Color

- Fragrance
- Shape
- Size

When you experiment with the above, it can be advantageous to try out different waxes and wicks to see what works best.

Each type of wax has its own melting point, pour temperature, fragrance load, and curing time, while different wicks are specific to the amount and type of wax used for the candle. You'll need to do your research and read about each wax and wick carefully to ensure that it fits your specific candle.

Essentially, there's a lot of trial and error that goes into customizing your candles, which is why we start with the basic recipe from chapter 1 first. Then, you can take your time creating your perfect custom candle, while your basic ones are already selling.

When creating your own candle, it's best to write down your ideas on a piece of paper and form an exact vision of who the candle is for, what you want it to smell/look like, and what your selling points will be.

Here are some questions to ask yourself, while brainstorming your custom candle:

- **What do you want the candle to look like?** (This will determine what type of candle you'll make, whether you'll use a container or a mold, the color and type of dye you'll use, etc.)
- **What do you want the candle to smell like?** (This will determine if you use fragrance or essential oils, which scent(s) you'll use, etc.)

- **How do you want the candle to make the customer feel?** (This will determine the general "aura" you want your candle to give off, such as relaxation, sleep, springtime, beach vibes, romance, etc.)
- **What are the selling points for your candle?** (This will determine the ideal customers for your candle and how you plan to sell it to them. This includes the name of the candle, which words you'll use to describe it, etc. We'll talk more about this later on.)
- **Is your candle on-brand for your business?** (For example, if your brand is all-natural candles then you'll want to use a sustainable wax, essential oils, and natural (or no) color. We'll dive further into branding later.)

If you can't come up with any ideas, feel free to look at candle making blogs, books, or websites for inspiration. You can also visit Yankee Candle, Etsy, or other stores that sell candles to get a sense of what's popular and selling well right now.

Here are some general themes that you can customize your candles around:

- Seasons
- Holidays
- Nature
- Travel
- Locations (such as countries, cities, landmarks, or US states)
- Trends
- Animals
- Fairytales
- Food
- Beach
- Flowers or gardens

- Relaxation (such as sleep, meditation, or yoga)
- Artistic or abstract
- Books, movies, or TV shows (just make there isn't an active copyright or trademark on the source material you're using—for example, you can't make and sell Harry Potter candles without permission from Warner Brothers because it's trademarked, BUT you may be able to make candles inspired by illustrations in Lewis Carroll's *Alice in Wonderland* since it's in the public domain; always do your research and even consider consulting with an attorney if you plan to do something like this)

Once you get the ideas flowing, the possibilities are truly endless! Write all your ideas down, so you can come back to them later.

Start with just one candle from your idea list and really flesh it out. Research the waxes, wicks, and other materials that will work best for this type of candle. Write down all the ingredients, equipment, and other items you'll need. It can also help to make a sketch of the candle, so that you have a visual reference to work from.

Once you've gathered all your research and materials, begin making your candle. Be sure to have a notebook and pen nearby, so you can record every step you take during the process. This ensures that you can recreate the candle later and makes it easy to identify changes that need to be made.

You should record:

- Temperature of the room
- All ingredients and equipment used
- All measurements (e.g., amount of fragrance oil used in ounces)
- Melting point and pour temperature

- How long the candle took to make
- Curing time
- Anything else that seems important or relevant (no detail is too small!)

Although your candle could turn out perfectly the first time, it will typically take two to five times to get it exactly right. This is why it's important to write down every detail, as you go through the process. It will allow you to identify what went wrong, make necessary changes, and keep track of it all as you go. Once you hit that perfect recipe, you'll already have it written down and can simply repeat it!

While there is definitely a learning curve with customizing your own candles, the process is also fun and exciting. Plus, once you have the recipe down correctly, you can simply rinse and repeat to add new candles to your inventory with ease.

Where to Start

We know this chapter has a lot of information, so here's a quick tutorial on how to get started customizing your candles:

1. As mentioned before, start with the basic candle from chapter 1 and create your first batch of inventory, changing only the fragrance at this stage. Keep practicing until your basic candle is perfect and you're starting to make sales.
2. When you decide it's time to start customizing your candles, begin with the basic candle and change just ONE simple element about it. For example, you could add color or choose a different type of container.
3. After this, you can advance to trying out different kinds of wax, mixing multiple fragrance oils, making a molded candle instead, and more.

4. Remember that practice makes progress. The more you experiment with making different candles, the faster you'll gain an understanding of what works and what doesn't work. Before long, you'll be a candle making pro!

Congrats! You're officially a candle making maven. In the following chapters, we'll discuss the business side of things and how to start making money from your creations.

CHAPTER 3

Let's Get Down to Business

Now that you have your inventory, it's time to explore the business side.

In this chapter, we'll teach you the basic business principles that are necessary for success in the candle industry. This will give you a general idea of the strategy and mindset you'll need to hit the ground running.

In later chapters, we'll provide a more detailed approach that covers exactly how to start and scale your business for massive growth and income.

Goals

Before you do anything else, it's important to set goals for your business. This will allow you to determine where you're starting from and what you'd like to achieve moving forward.

You'll want to set specific and measurable goals that can be realistically achieved within a set period of time (e.g., a month, a quarter, or a year).

There are three types of goals that we recommend setting for your business:

1. Task Goals

These are goals related to a specific task, such as starting a YouTube channel or adding a new scent line to your business.

2. Strategy Goals

These are goals related to an overall strategy for your business and often need to be broken down into smaller, actionable steps.

Here's an example:

Goal: Expand visibility for my business

Action steps:

- Create a business website
- Create a LinkedIn Page
- Run a daily ad on Pinterest

It can also be helpful to have a timeline for each action step.

3. Numerical Goals

These are goals that are measured in specific numbers. Examples include: make $1,000 a month, expand customer base by 30%, or have 500 followers on Pinterest.

You should plan to review and redefine your goals every quarter, or three months, to make sure that you're on track. This will also allow you to determine if certain goals need to be modified.

Don't be discouraged if you don't meet all your goals within the set time frame. The purpose behind setting goals isn't necessarily to achieve them all, but rather to create a clear path for your business to move forward.

If your goal was to have 100 subscribers on your email list by the end of the first quarter and you only have 60, you should still celebrate this as a victory because you started from zero. Then, you can reset your goal to 120 subscribers by the end of the second quarter knowing that you're already halfway there.

One of our favorite quotes is, "Shoot for the moon. Even if you miss, you'll land among the stars." It's a reminder that any amount of progress gets you closer to success.

Finally, keep in mind that your goals will not be static. They will shift over time as you grow, progress, and achieve milestones in your business.

Research

With any business, it's important to do research, understand the industry, and know your competitors. The business world is never static, so it's essential to always stay up to date and in the know.

This is as simple as periodically doing a quick search for "candles" on platforms, such as Google, Amazon, Etsy, Pinterest, or Instagram. At a glance, you'll be able to see what's popular, what's selling (and what's not selling), who your competitors are, and more.

Next, search for websites or blogs that are specific to candle making or candle businesses. Sign up for the newsletters of anything that looks interesting, so you can stay ahead of the market and changing trends.

Here are some candle making resources that we recommend:

National Candle Association
Candlefind
Armatage Candle Company Blog

Just a few hours of this kind of research makes a huge difference to your success in the candle making business. The more you understand the industry, its key players, and its customers, the more effectively you'll be able to sell your candles.

Niche

Every successful business starts with a niche. A niche is simply the market segment that's MOST interested in purchasing your type of products. This is often narrowed down to a subniche that encompasses a smaller, but more specific, segment of the market.

The more specific your niche is, the easier it will be to sell your candles. The key here is simply to find a segment of the candle market that's large enough to have a substantial customer base, but small enough that you can still stand out.

The most profitable niches have a demand that's higher than the competition. The research detailed in the previous section will help you determine which niches are popular without being saturated.

Here are examples of candle niches:

- General: luxury, natural, artistic
- Scents: beach, flowers, dessert
- Themes: yoga, bakery, literature
- Customer type: busy mom, bargain shopper, high-end spa

Keep in mind that the above are just general niches to get your juices flowing. The more you can niche down, the better.

You can even combine several niches to create a subniche. For example, instead of just luxury candles, you could make luxury spa candles with your target audience being high-end hotels, day spas, or saunas, as well as customers who want to make their homes smell like a luxury spa experience.

In addition to market research, think about the type of customer you want to reach and how you want your candles to make them feel. Also consider what you're passionate about, skilled at, or interested in.

As an example, D'Shawn Russell of Southern Elegance, found success in the candle industry by choosing a unique niche that she's passionate about: candles with Southern-inspired fragrances.

Her candles are specifically designed to evoke memories of simpler times, small-town living, and childhood nostalgia with many candles being named after a Southern city. Each of her candles tells a story, bringing warmth and comfort to a specific type of customer.

While Ms. Russell's candles certainly won't appeal to everyone, there is a large enough segment of the market that LOVES her candles for her business to be highly profitable. In fact, her business currently earns $1.6 million a year.

This familiar expression sums it up: "When you speak to everyone, you speak to no one." If you want to be successful in business, you need to speak to a specific customer base and drown out the rest.

Even when you're just starting out with your basic candles in three to four different scents (see chapter 1), it helps to already have a general niche in mind and attempt to choose scents and containers that align with that niche. Then, later on, you can niche down even further, as you start to customize your candles.

Keep in mind that your niche could evolve over time, as you move away from basic candles and learn to customize. This is totally fine! You don't need to have your niche completely nailed down in order to open your business.

As always, our goal is to get you selling first. This not only propels your business off the ground faster, but also allows you to perform much-needed market research. You can always refine your niche later, as you learn what resonates best with your customers!

Ideal Customer

When choosing a niche, you'll need to identify your ideal customer. This is the main type of customer you're trying to reach through your business.

Your ideal customer will be at the heart of every decision you'll make moving forward, including branding, pricing, social media channels, and much more.

In order to effectively market your candles, you'll need to picture your ideal customer as a real person and home in on their needs, wants, or desires. In other words, your customer has a problem and you're providing the solution.

Here are some questions to ask yourself:

- Who is your ideal customer? Nail down some basics like gender, marital status, kids, income, etc. This can obviously be fluid, but will help solidify the image of your ideal customer in your mind.

- Where does your ideal customer shop? What are some of their favorite shops?
- What social media channels does your ideal customer spend the most time on?
- What blogs or websites does your ideal customer visit?
- What does your ideal customer like to do in their free time?
- What does your ideal customer spend money on (besides the essentials like food and housing)? How much are they willing to spend on these nonessentials?

Think through these questions fully and write your answers down. It will be helpful to refer back to this periodically as a reminder of who your business is for and how you can better serve them.

Customer Service

Customer service is at the forefront of any six-figure business. If your business is lacking in this area, it will be difficult to maintain repeat or consistent sales.

When opening your candle business, customer satisfaction automatically becomes a top priority. It's important to build trust and loyalty with buyers, as you literally can't make money without them.

Here are some tips for providing excellent customer service:

- *Be responsive.* You should always respond to customer inquiries in a timely manner, preferably within 24 hours on weekdays and first thing Monday morning after weekends.
- *Be personable.* While you should always be polite and professional when interacting with customers, don't be afraid

to show off your personality. Especially when it comes to small shops, customers like to see the "real person" behind the business.

- *Be transparent.* Always be honest with customers. Never try to cover up a mistake or set unreasonable expectations. If something goes wrong on your end, simply apologize and provide a solution.
- *Be level-headed.* Never get emotional or argue with customers. Remember that this is business and interactions with customers should never be taken personally. While it can sting when a customer is unhappy, always strive to be professional and keep a level head.

Congrats! You've just completed Business 101 and now you're ready to open up shop.

CHAPTER 4

Start Selling

You have candles in hand and business principles in mind, so now you're ready to sell, sell, SELL! But, where to start?

In this chapter, we'll explore the primary ways to sell your candles and grow your six-figure business. We'll share basic tips for getting started, alongside pros and cons for each option, so you can make an educated decision about which one(s) will work best for you.

Etsy

Our number one platform for selling candles from home is Etsy. It's hands down the easiest way to start selling and get your business off the ground quickly.

Etsy is a global online marketplace that focuses on handmade, vintage, and craft items. This means a built-in customer base that's already primed to buy your homemade candles.

You don't need a storefront or even a website to be successful on Etsy. Etsy is a growing marketplace of 96.3 million active buyers, so with the right strategies in place, your ideal customers will come straight to you!

If you only sell your candles on one platform, Etsy should be the one. Many sellers make full-time six- or even seven-figure incomes just by selling on Etsy.

Even if you've never used the Etsy platform before, you can set up your shop in just five minutes and begin selling right away. Faster setup equals faster income.

To open your shop, go to Etsy.com/sell. Once you choose your shop name, put up your first listing, and share payment details, you're ready to start selling. It really is that easy!

Once you open your shop, you'll find that Etsy has many built-in tools to help sellers succeed, such as marketing, analytics, and much more. You can customize your online storefront, print shipping labels (with discounts), and manage all the day-to-day operations for your shop directly from the platform. You'll find all of these user-friendly tools in the Shop Manager.

If you'd like a more in-depth guide on how to successfully run a profitable business on Etsy, we highly recommend our other book, *Etsy Business Launch: The Complete Guide to Making Six Figures Selling on Etsy*. It was designed as a companion to this book and is a surefire way to supercharge your results!

While it's easy to get started on Etsy, the strategies needed for success could fill an entire book (literally!) Etsy is a highly competitive platform with lots of sellers and a bit of a learning curve. You'll need a full understanding of Etsy's algorithm, marketing, and strategies in order to bring the right customers to your shop. In *Etsy Business Launch*, we share the exact framework needed to grow your business, boost sales, and create a full-time income through the Etsy platform.

We recommend that ALL novice candle sellers start with Etsy first. This is the quickest and simplest way to get your candle business off to a strong start. Then later on, when your Etsy shop is well established and making consistent income, you can explore adding another option from this list to your business model, if you want to.

Pros:

- Easy to set up
- High income potential
- Worldwide market
- Largest marketplace for creative businesses
- Self-contained (everything you need to run your shop is located within the platform itself)
- Already has a built-in customer base, which allows you to make money faster than starting an independent online business or brick-and-mortar store from scratch
- Marketing tools, analytics, Etsy support, discounted shipping labels, and more

Cons:

- Competitive platform with lots of sellers
- Requires more in-depth knowledge to stand out in your niche
- Etsy fees, advertising fees, and payment processing fees cut into your profit

Facebook Marketplace

Facebook Marketplace has quickly climbed the ranks since it was established in 2016. Similar to Craigslist, Facebook Marketplace allows users to sell locally through local pickup. It also offers the added bonus of nationwide shipping, where the seller ships directly to the buyer.

Facebook comes with the distinct advantage of its massive user base with 2.9 billion monthly active users and an estimated one billion monthly marketplace users.

It's also super easy to set up—all you need is a Facebook account. From there, you just click on Marketplace and then Sell. Add your title, price, category, and photos then you're ready to go!

While Facebook Marketplace is growing in popularity with e-commerce businesses and entrepreneurs, it's still largely seen as a clearinghouse for people's used or unwanted items (think: Craigslist). As such, it can be harder to gain traction as a professional business, if you're only using Facebook Marketplace.

Overall, Facebook Marketplace isn't our favorite platform for building a full-time candle business. However, if you're only looking to make a part-time income OR if you're only interested in selling locally then you could definitely build your business using just this one platform.

Otherwise, we recommend using Facebook Marketplace in addition to one of the other options listed in this chapter. It can bring extra money into your business, but shouldn't be relied on as your only source of income.

Pros:

- Huge platform with one billion monthly marketplace users
- Very easy to set up, especially if you already have a Facebook account
- Zero fees if you sell locally

Cons:

- More difficult to gain traction and achieve consistent sales
- Often associated with getting rid of used items rather than a platform for legitimate businesses (this could change over time)
- Standard selling fees for shipped orders cut into your profit

Business Website

Another way to sell your candles online is to establish an independent business where you sell through your own website, rather than relying on an already established platform, such as Etsy or Facebook Marketplace.

If you want to start your own online business website, you'll first need a domain name and web hosting. A domain name is simply the URL for your business (e.g., yogacandles.com). You can check the availability of your chosen domain name by going to namecheap.com and entering it into the search bar.

Web hosting is the process of renting space online for your website. There are many inexpensive options for this, such as Bluehost or SiteGround. You'll also need to add a payment gateway, which connects your website to a checkout system, such as Stripe or Square.

If you have no experience building or running your own website, there will definitely be a steep learning curve here. You may need a professional to set up your website for you, which can be costly.

The biggest advantage of this approach is that you'll be in full control of your online candle business. You won't be subject to Etsy or Facebook algorithms, selling fees, or anything else. You run your business on your own terms.

The major downside is that it's much harder to gain traction this way. While Etsy and Facebook Marketplace come with fees and other caveats, these are in exchange for access to their large, built-in customer bases, as well as other tools that help sellers succeed. The users on this platform are already primed to buy and have trust in the platform itself.

It's much easier to make quick and consistent sales when you have a customer base already available to you rather than starting completely from scratch. It takes time to gain the attention and trust of potential customers, so earning a full-time income from your candles will likely take longer.

Another downside is that Etsy and Facebook are free to set up and charge nominal fees for selling on their platform. If you build your own online business, there will be more costs up front to set up and maintain your website, resulting in a bit more financial risk. Payment gateways (such as, Stripe or Square) also come with their own transaction fees, so there's no way to avoid those entirely.

Overall, we recommend starting with Etsy first and then later on, once you have a solid customer base, you can sell through your own website as well. Etsy even has a website option called Pattern by Etsy that syncs with your Etsy shop and allows further customization.

Pros:

- Complete control over your own business, website, and sales
- More opportunity for customization and adding your own unique style and flair

Cons:

- Much harder for new business owners to gain traction and consistent sales
- More up-front costs
- Steeper learning curve
- More risk

Brick and Mortar

A brick-and-mortar store operates conventionally instead of over the Internet. It's a retail store, where customers can shop and buy items in person.

Although e-commerce sales are consistently growing, many customers still prefer to buy in-store. There's definitely a sense of pride in having a tangible store that customers can visit. That being said, a brick-and-mortar store comes with a large amount of risk.

While an online business can be set up in a few days with only a little capital, a brick-and-mortar store comes with longer timelines and major startup costs. You'll need to find a suitable building and then secure at least two years of financing for rent. You'll also need licenses, permits, store fixtures and equipment, property insurance, and much more.

While an online business can typically be run by just one person, a retail store requires hiring staff, such as cashiers, cleaning crew, and more. In addition to this, you'll still want to have a website, so you can sell your items nationwide.

Unless a brick-and-mortar store is the ultimate dream for you (and you have the funds to make it work), we HIGHLY recommend starting an online business through Etsy, Facebook, or your own website instead. This will allow you to set up shop quickly, run your business from home, and make money faster.

Online options have much lower startup costs and, therefore, very little risk compared to a physical store. There's always the option to add physical stores later on, if your online shop really blows up!

Pros:

- Many customers still prefer to shop in-store
- Sense of pride in having your own physical storefront
- Generally less competition than online

Cons:

- High risk
- High capital
- Much longer timeline for making back your initial investment and turning a profit

Farmers Markets and Craft Fairs

Another popular option for candle businesses is to sell at farmers markets or craft fairs. If you're an outgoing person, who loves being around people, this option can be a lot of fun and very rewarding.

To sell at a farmers market, you'll typically need a permit and a booth. Be sure to research the requirements pertaining to your state or country beforehand.

Many farmers markets have waiting lists for a booth, so get on this early, if you're interested. Most markets have a website, where you can apply online to be a vendor.

While selling at these venues won't make you a millionaire, it's a great option for those who want to make a part-time income selling candles locally and in person. Farmers markets typically only take place on the weekend, which allows you to focus on other ventures during the week.

They're also a great way to earn extra income, in addition to an Etsy shop or another option on this list. You can even bring flyers for your Etsy shop to the farmers market to encourage online business as well.

Pros:

- A fun environment to interact with customers directly
- Can make a part-time income with just a few hours a week (after initial set up)
- Can be used to promote your Etsy shop or online store

Cons:

- The need for permits, licenses, and an available booth could slow down your timeline for making an income
- Not great for those who want to make a full-time or six-figure income

At this point, you should have some inspiration for where you want to sell your candles. Any of these options can work depending on what speaks most to you and the income level you'd like to achieve. Just remember to be practical about how much time, energy, and funds you're able to put into your business to start.

If you want to scale to six figures quickly with just one platform, we do recommend Etsy first and foremost. The startup costs are low and you can always add other options from this list later on.

CHAPTER 5

It's All About Your Brand

In this chapter, we'll explore one of the most important aspects of a six-figure business: branding. Every successful business has a distinct brand that separates it from its competitors.

What separates a Nike shoe from a generic sneaker? Or Coca-Cola from Pepsi? Why do so many people spend thousands of dollars on a MacBook Pro, when they can get an HP laptop for a few hundred? It's largely the brand itself and the loyalty it inspires from its customers.

If you want to be successful selling candles, it's up to you to create a brand that stands out in the market. Anyone can stock a candle, but what makes your candle different?

As long as your candle is well-made and high-quality, it isn't the product itself that makes sales, but rather the branding. This is your most powerful marketing tool.

Throughout this section, think about your basic candles from chapter 1 and how you can use branding to capture a specific segment of the market.

What's in a Brand?

Think about your niche and the ideal customer you identified in chapter 3. Your branding should clearly communicate, beyond a shadow of a doubt, that your business is for them.

This means that everything from your marketing materials to the candles themselves needs to speak directly to this ONE customer base. There needs to be consistency throughout your business with the singular goal of attracting this one type of ideal customer.

Here's how to do this:

1. Business or Shop Name

For starters, the name of your business should be aligned with your brand, so the right customers can find you.

For example, while Candles by Carrie is a nice name, it doesn't communicate at all the types of candles that Carrie sells. By contrast, Yoga Candles gives us a much clearer idea of who these particular candles are for and what customers can expect.

In reference to our example from chapter 3, D'Shawn Russell's business is called Southern Elegance Candle Company. Since all of her candles are Southern-inspired, this name will bring a mass of ideal customers right to her website!

2. Logo

Every business should have a logo that reflects its brand. In designing your logo, you should choose fonts, colors, and elements that align with your niche and ideal customer.

For example, if your niche is candles with beach scents then a logo with a wave, sunshine, or sandcastle would be perfectly on-brand. If instead, your focus is spa candles then relaxing colors like pastel blue or lavender would draw your ideal customer right in.

Your logo can be professionally designed (search for logo designers online or check Fiverr for affordable options) or you can create your own using a graphic design tool like Canva or PicMonkey. Just make sure your logo is clean, appealing, and, of course, on-brand.

This is where market research comes in handy. You can search Pinterest boards for inspiration, look at other logos (just don't copy them), or research trends in your niche.

3. Color Palette and Fonts

It's important to have a consistent color palette and fonts for all your business and marketing materials. Whether you're creating flyers, business cards, or graphics for social media, you want customers who are familiar with your business to identify your brand at a glance.

Choose colors and fonts that are congruent with your niche. For example, if you sell floral candles, then elegant fonts and spring colors will pop the most for your ideal customer.

Decide on a few fonts and colors that match your brand the best and use them consistently throughout all elements of your business.

4. Style

Every brand has a unique style that will shine through in your photos, copy, website, and more. As with the other elements on this list, choose a style that resonates with your brand and use it consistently.

Use the same backdrop and styling for photos. Write descriptions that pop and make sense for your niche. Choose packaging and promotional materials that reflect your ideal customer. This is all part of creating a brand.

In summary, when it comes to branding, it should always be clear what kinds of candles you sell and who your target market is. This is your best form of advertisement and will draw the right customers directly to you.

What's in a Name?

Another important aspect of branding, particularly in the candle industry, is the names you choose for your candles and scents.

Think about this: While there are thousands of rose candles on the market, you could be one of the few selling a "Portland Rose Garden" candle. It's the exact same scent—just different branding.

Those who have fond memories of June afternoons spent in the Portland Rose Garden will feel a strong pull toward your candle and are, therefore, very likely to make a purchase. With candles, customers are often purchasing a feeling more so than a physical product.

While not every person searching for a rose candle will be interested in a Portland Rose Garden candle, the ones who are will flock right to you. You'll be much more likely to make a sale this way than attempting to stand out in a massive sea of just "rose" candles.

Candles are all about eliciting a specific memory, emotional response, or feeling. Choose names that are enticing, comforting, or evocative. For example, "Sunrise at the Beach" conjures a much more vivid and specific memory than simply "Ocean."

This also extends to the sales description for your candles. What sounds more inviting? "This soy candle is pink and smells like rose" or "This candle will transport you to an English garden filled with fresh pink blooms and the promise of eternal spring."

In short, the more of an emotional response you can obtain from your ideal customers, the more candles you'll sell. As discussed in chapter 1, your candles can be very simple, as long as the name and branding capture the essence of how your customers want to FEEL when they light them. Be creative and do some research on popular trends within your niche to maximize sales.

Keep in mind that you're competing with Yankee Candle and other major candle retailers for sales. You need to give customers a specific reason to purchase your candle over any other. This all comes down to branding. The more you home in on this, the more successful your business will be.

CHAPTER 6

Perfect Packaging

In this chapter, we'll discuss labels, packaging, and shipping. Note that packaging is part of branding as well, so be sure to keep your ideal customer in mind throughout this section.

Labels

There are two types of labels that you're required to have on the candle itself. The first is a brand label, which you'll adhere to the front of the candle. The second is a warning label, which you'll adhere to the bottom.

Please note that the guidance in this section is for US candles only. If you plan to sell candles in a different country, you'll need to research those labeling requirements instead.

In the United States, the Fair Packaging and Labeling Act (FPLA) has detailed requirements for candle labels. Before we get started, please note that we are not legal professionals and this is not legal advice.

You should check the Federal Trade Commission (FTC), Consumer Product Safety Commission (CPSC), and National Candle Association (NCA) websites to ensure you're complying with the latest requirements and guidelines. Do your research and consult with a legal professional, if you have any questions or concerns.

The first required label is a brand label, which you'll adhere to the front of the candle. On round candles, this label should cover 40% of the surface, while on rectangular candles, they should cover one side.

Here's what the brand label should include:

- *Statement of identity* (required) – This is simply what the product is (scented candle, candle, wax melt, etc.) While this may seem obvious, it's a legal requirement, so make sure you state the product prominently and explicitly.

- *Company's name, contact information, and logo* (required) – Only the town and state of the company are required, as long as other contact information is present (like a phone number and website address). Even if this wasn't a requirement, you would want this anyway for branding and marketing purposes.

- *Weight* (required) – Display the product's weight in both standard and metric measurements. This should be the entire weight of the finished candle, including wax and wick. There is a minimum required font height for this information that depends on the size of your label. If your label is:
  o Less than or equal to 5 square inches = 1/16 inch font
  o 5 to 25 square inches = 1/8 inch font
  o 25 to 100 square inches = 3/16 inch font

- *Candle name* (optional, but HIGHLY recommended) – This is not legally required, but obviously you'll want to put the name of your candle on the label.

- *Wax type and scent* (optional) – This is not strictly required, but considered an industry standard.

- *Method of production* (optional) – Also not required, but nice to have. An example of this would be "hand-poured" or "handcrafted."

- *Burn time* (optional) – Once again, not required but helpful to the consumer. This is the amount of time the candle will burn in hours.

In addition to the required information, this label should match your brand in terms of font, colors, and graphics. Your labels should also be heat-resistant and able to sustain extreme temperature changes without damage.

You can create custom heat-resistant labels on stickeryou.com or lightninglabels.com. Alternatively, you can create your own brand label using a graphic design tool like Canva (this option is more work at first, but will save money in the long run). Regardless of what you choose, just be sure that your labels are safe for candles.

An example of a brand label would be like this:

Yoga Candles

Hotel Spa Day
Scented Candle

Hand-Poured in Berkeley, California

Soy Wax Blend
Lavender + Jasmine + Eucalyptus
Approx. 50-Hour Burn Time

9.0 oz (255 g)

Made in the USA
yogacandles.com

The second label you'll need is a warning label. This is a voluntary guideline established by the National Candle Association (NCA) and is considered an industry standard.

Here's what the warning label should include:

- Burn within sight
- Keep away from combustibles
- Keep away from children

The NCA has graphic safety symbols available on their website that you can add to your candles as well. This is not required, but recommended, as they present a visual safety reminder.

Your warning label can also include optional safety information, such as:

- Do not burn candle for more than 4 hours at a time.
- Trim wick to ¼ inch before every lighting.
- Place on fireproof surface and keep away from drafts.

This warning label is typically adhered to the bottom of the candle. Once again, just be sure the label is heat-resistant.

Packaging

If you're selling on Etsy or any of the other e-commerce platforms outlined in chapter 4, you'll need to package your candles for shipping. This section will help you choose the right packaging for your brand, while also ensuring that your items arrive safely to your customers.

While not strictly necessary, it is ideal to package your candle in a product box, such as a cardboard tube. This is especially true for pillar candles or other candles that don't have their own container.

You can find paper candle tubes at most candle supply stores, such as candlescience.com. Alternatively, you can use a square or rectangular cardboard box. (Note that the product box isn't the same one that you'll ship the candle in. It's a smaller box designed to hold just the candle itself.)

Your product box is also a great opportunity for branding. You can design custom boxes to fit your brand using services, such as packola.com or noissue.co. Otherwise, you can use plain boxes and add a branded sticker that has your logo or business name on it. Just be sure to measure your candle to confirm that it will fit properly in the box or tube.

If you'd rather not purchase product boxes to start, you can wrap your candles in tissue paper instead and then affix branded stickers or regular tape to the closure. You can choose colored or printed tissue paper that fits your brand—just make sure the colors won't bleed onto your candle.

Once your candle is in the product box or tissue paper, we recommend also wrapping it in a layer of bubble wrap for extra protection before shipping. This is especially necessary for fragile items, such as container candles in glass vessels.

Next, you'll choose a shipping box that leaves about 1–2 inches of room around your candle(s) for packing material. To choose the right shipping box, you'll need to measure the candle once it's already packaged, so you can pick a box with the right dimensions. It's helpful to have a variety of box sizes available for customers who order multiple candles.

Once you've chosen your box, add about 1–2 inches of packing material to the bottom. You can use packing paper or tissue paper for regular products and biodegradable packing peanuts for fragile products.

Place the candle(s) into the box and add 1–2 inches of packing material to both sides and on top. This process ensures that your candles fit snugly, reducing the chance of breakage. Always check to make sure that your candle isn't touching the sides of the box. If you're shipping multiple candles, add a bit of packing material in between to prevent any damage caused by them knocking against each other.

Make sure that your box is taped down securely with packing tape on all sides. You can use two layers of packing tape, if needed.

Once your box is packed, you'll need to weigh it and then print a shipping label. We'll discuss this further in the next section.

To review, here's a list of the basic shipping materials you'll need:

- Product box or tissue paper
- Branded stickers or regular tape (colored or clear)
- Bubble wrap
- Shipping box
- Packing material (packing paper, tissue paper, or biodegradable packing peanuts)
- Packing tape
- Shipping label
- Tape measure
- Scale
- Printer, ink, and paper (for printing shipping labels)

Most of the above items can be purchased at office supplies stores, such as Office Depot, or online at Amazon or Uline. USPS also offers free boxes for certain shipping services, which we'll discuss in the next section.

Shipping

Now that your candle is snug in its box and ready to find its new home, let's talk shipping!

The cost to ship your candles will be determined by the size of your shipping box (most boxes will have dimensions listed at the bottom) and the total weight of your packaged item, as well as the shipping point, origin, and speed.

Before you ship your package, you'll need to weigh it and print a shipping label. In terms of weighing your item, a digital shipping scale or a kitchen scale will work best. If push comes to shove, you can use a regular bathroom or body weight scale.

If you're selling on Etsy, you'll be able to print a discounted shipping label directly through the platform. They offer a choice between FedEx and USPS for sellers located in the US.

If you live outside the US, there are many available options for shipping on Etsy, including Canada Post, Royal Mail, Australia Post, Global Postal Shipping, and more, depending on where you're based.

USPS Priority Mail is a great option for shipping candles within the United States. It's cost-effective, insured, and you can save money by using free Priority Mail shipping boxes. You can pick these up at the post office or order them online at usps.com. Just be sure that you only use these boxes for USPS Priority Mail.

If you're not selling through Etsy, Pirate Ship is a licensed e-commerce platform that also offers discounts on USPS shipping.

In either case, you'll input both the size and weight of your package to produce your shipping label. Once it's printed, you can affix it to the top of your package with clear packing tape and you're ready to go!

Who Pays?

There are two options when it comes to paying for shipping. The first is the buyer pays for shipping separately, in addition to the cost of the candle. The second is the seller (that's you) pays for shipping and builds it into the cost of the candle itself, which is referred to as "free shipping."

We highly recommend offering free shipping, as customers tend to love it, perceiving it as a better deal. It gives the impression that they're receiving something for free with their purchase, as opposed to getting to the checkout page and having to spend extra money on shipping. If you're selling on Etsy, free shipping can even give your listings a boost in search results.

And don't worry! You won't lose money on this. Instead, you'll just factor the cost of shipping into the price of the candle itself (we'll discuss this more in the next chapter.) The customer will feel like they're getting a free perk, while in reality, the cost of shipping is already covered by their purchase. It's a win-win!

Another option is to offer free shipping with a certain order amount (e.g., free shipping over $50 or free shipping for two or more candles). Either one of these methods will encourage more business for your candle store.

Package Tips

Here are a few items you can include in your package to increase sales and encourage repeat business:

1. Thank You Note

Every package should include a thank you note. This can be a printed card or even a handwritten note that aligns with your brand.

A simple "Thanks for making a purchase!" or "Thank you for supporting a small business" can make a huge difference in terms of customer loyalty. It's a small gesture that can lead to repeat sales.

In this note or card, you can also ask for a review, encourage them to follow you on social media, or offer a discount on their next purchase.

2. Coupon

In addition to a thank you note, a coupon is a great way to encourage repeat business. We recommend including a coupon in each package for 10% off the customer's next order. Set an expiration date that's about 30–60 days out, so they don't forget to use it.

3. Free Sample

Another great sales tool is free samples. When you're selling candles online, it can be hard for customers to fully understand the scent profile.

Once you become adept at making candles, you can easily create small, scented tea light candles alongside your larger ones to include in packages as samples. You'll just need a bit of extra wax, wicks, and some small containers. It's best to make 3–5 different sample tea lights in your most popular scents.

You can include one sample tea light per order as a free gift. Be sure to advertise this on your listing or website, as this can encourage orders as well (e.g., FREE scented tealight with every purchase!).

All of the above contribute to repeat customers, which is a great way to grow your business. Research shows that by increasing customer retention by just 5 percent, a business's profitability can increase by a whopping 75%!

This is because repeat customers will shop with you more often and spend more with each purchase. They're a reliable source of income and should be treated as your most loyal VIP customers.

CHAPTER 7

Pro Pricing

Now that you have the perfect package, let's explore pricing!

What should you charge for your candles? The traditional metric is to charge three to four times your cost for direct sale and two times your cost for wholesale.

Direct sale is when you sell your product directly to consumers (i.e., a customer buys a candle from your store), while wholesale is when you, as the supplier, sell products in bulk to a retailer (i.e., you sell 100 of your candles to a store and THEY sell the candle to the customer).

If you choose one of the selling options in chapter 4, you will mostly sell direct, but you may occasionally get a request for a wholesale order, where you'll offer a significant discount for a bulk purchase. For the purpose of this chapter, we'll focus on pricing for direct sales, since that's where the vast majority of new candle sellers will start.

Candlescience.com recommends the following price ranges for a 5.8-ounce candle based on each market type:

- Mass market: $7 to $11
- Mid-market or "niche": $13 to $18
- High-end or "prestige": $19 to $28+

As an independent business selling handmade goods, your candles will generally fall into the "mid-market" category. However, if you sell luxury or spa candles, your products could fall into the "high-end" category.

While the above metrics are helpful guidelines, there are many factors that come into play when it comes to pricing, including costs, branding, target market, discounts, and more.

Also, keep in mind that in the candle industry, cheaper does not necessarily mean more sales. You're selling a unique, handmade item and the right customers expect to pay more for a product like this.

While you obviously don't want to gouge your customers, you don't have to undercharge in an attempt to make a sale. It's all about finding the right balance between what your items are worth and what your customers are willing to pay.

Costs

When it comes to pricing your candles, the most important factor is your costs. There are two costs to consider: variable and fixed. You must calculate these ahead of time to ensure you'll make a profit.

Variable Cost

Variable cost accounts for each individual component of a candle, including production, packaging, and shipping. These expenses vary based on how many candles you make.

When calculated, you will know the exact cost of each candle in a batch. This can vary for each type of candle you sell, if the size or components are different.

For example, an 8-ounce candle will have a different variable cost than a 4-ounce candle. Even if the two candles use the same ingredients, different quantities will be used for each one, resulting in separate variable costs.

In order to calculate variable cost, you'll need the exact cost of every ingredient used for a batch of candles and the amount used for each candle. This is why it's important to always write down specifics as you're going through the candle making process.

Let's say you're making a batch of twenty-five 5.8-ounce scented paraffin container candles. Here's how you would calculate the variable cost per candle:

If the paraffin wax is $1.20 per pound then you would first convert this to the cost per ounce. There are 16 ounces in a pound, so you would divide $1.20 by 16 to get the cost per ounce of $0.08 (this number is rounded up from 0.075). Then, you would multiply $0.08 by 5.8 ounces to get $0.46. This means the cost of paraffin wax per 5.8-ounce candle is $0.46.

If you use 0.50 ounces of fragrance oil per candle and the fragrance oil costs $1.15 per ounce then you would multiply 0.50 by $1.15 to get the cost per candle of $0.58.

Another cost you'll want to factor in is the cost of shipping the materials to you. Note that this is different from the cost of shipping to your customer, which we'll calculate later. If you ordered all your candle materials from candlescience.com and paid $20 for shipping then you would simply divide $20 by 25 (the number of candles in the batch) and add $0.80 for shipping to the cost of each candle.

When you purchase items like wicks, jars, and labels, there will typically be a per-item cost listed. If not, you can make a quick calculation by dividing the cost by the number of units. For example, if you purchase twelve jars for $5, the cost per jar will be $5 divided by 12 or $0.42. If you purchase 1,000 warning labels for $39.90, the cost per label will be $39.90 divided by 1,000 or $0.04.

Using the calculations shown above, here's the complete list of what the materials for our example candle amount to:

Paraffin wax: $0.46
Fragrance oil: $0.58
Wick: $0.08
Wick sticker: $0.02
Jar: $0.42
Lid: $0.18
Warning label: $0.04
Brand label: $0.38
Shipping (for supplies): $0.80
Total: $2.96

After you calculate the cost of materials for the candle itself, you'll want to calculate the cost of packaging and shipping, if applicable.

This includes the cost of the shipping materials discussed in chapter 6, such as product boxes, shipping boxes, tissue paper, bubble wrap, shipping labels, and anything else you're using to package your candles.

Similar to the example above, you'll need to figure out the per-item cost of your materials. For example, if you purchase 100 sheets of tissue paper for $7.99, the cost per sheet is $7.99 divided by 100 or $0.08. If you use two sheets to wrap each candle then the cost per candle for tissue paper will be $0.16.

Here's another example. If bubble wrap costs $0.15 per square foot and you use three square feet, it will cost $0.15 multiplied by 3 or $0.45 per candle.

Also be sure to note the shipping costs for your packaging materials (the cost of them being shipped to you), if applicable. Just like above, divide the cost of shipping for packaging materials by the number of candles you're able to package using those materials.

Here's the cost of shipping materials for our example candle:

Product box: $1.20
Shipping box: $0.49
Packing paper: $0.10
Tape: $0.03
Shipping: $0.40
Total: $2.22

Finally, you'll add the variable costs together:

$2.96 (total for candle materials) + $2.22 (total for shipping materials) = $5.18 (total variable cost of your candle)

For some of these costs, you may need to use estimates. Just be sure to always estimate HIGH, so you won't take a loss later. Also note that if you're offering free shipping, the cost of shipping will need to be factored in as well.

While this calculation process can be a bit tedious at first (especially if, like us, math isn't your favorite subject), it'll become much easier over time as your costs become standard. If you ever get frustrated during this process, just remember that it's worth it to ensure you're making the BEST profit per candle that you possibly can.

No one wants to take a loss on their business, right? Taking the time to do these calculations beforehand ensures that you won't.

Fixed Cost

Fixed costs are standard for every product you sell. Examples of fixed costs are insurance, listing fees, email or graphic design platforms, advertising fees, and more.

These are costs that pertain to your business as a whole, and not just the materials used to make and package your candles. These costs remain constant, no matter how many candles you make. They will typically be yearly or monthly fees.

Divide the monthly cost of these expenses by the average number of candles you make in a month to get the fixed cost per candle.

For example, if your small business insurance costs $42 per month and you make approximately 100 candles per month, the fixed cost of your insurance will be $42 divided by 100 or $0.42 per candle.

Another example is if you pay $9 per month for your email marketing platform and make approximately 100 candles per month, the fixed cost per candle will be $9 divided by 100 or $0.09.

Another fixed cost to consider is labor. You need to pay yourself first, right? A good range to start is $10–$15 per hour.

So, if it takes you 1.5 hours of active work (don't include curing time) to make one batch of 25 candles and you're paying yourself $12 an hour, you'll first multiply $12 by 1.5 to get $18 and then divide that by 25 to get $0.72 per candle for labor.

Here are the fixed costs for our example candle:

Insurance: $0.42
Labor: $0.72
Listing fee: $0.20
Email marketing platform: $0.09
Total fixed cost: $1.43

Total Cost

Here, you'll add up your variable and fixed costs per candle.

From our previous examples:

$$\$5.18 \text{ (total variable cost of your candle)} +$$
$$\$1.43 \text{ (total fixed cost)} = \$6.61$$

This means $6.61 is the total cost to make, package, and sell your candle!

Markup

Now that you have the cost, how do you decide on pricing? We'll start by adding a standard markup.

Markup is simply the amount added to your item's price that reflects profit after all variable and fixed costs are accounted for. It's represented as a percentage of your item's total cost, anywhere from 15% to 60%. In general, 30%–40% is the sweet spot for new candle businesses.

We'll add a 30% markup to our previous total cost of $6.61 by multiplying $6.61 by 1.30 to receive a total price of $8.59 for your candle.

This is just a start though. In the next step, we'll analyze the price of $8.59 within your target market to receive a final price.

Target Market

Now that you have a starting price of $8.59, it's time to adjust the price to your target market. Target market is basically another term for your ideal customer base—the segment of the market that is most likely to buy your products.

As mentioned in the introduction of this book, while a standard retail markup might be just 30%–60%, it's not uncommon for candles to sell for three to four times their cost. We'll achieve this profit margin by returning to our target market.

As noted previously, candlescience.com recommends the following price ranges for a 5.8-ounce candle based on each market type:

- Mass market: $7 to $11
- Mid-market or "niche": $13 to $18
- High-end or "prestige": $19 to $28+

Our price of $8.59 is definitely on the low side for a niche market and can be increased to hit the $13 to $18 range or even the $19 to $28 range, if it's a luxury candle.

Your final price should most directly correlate with WHO is buying your candle and WHERE you're selling it. This is once again, where we return to market research.

As an example, if you're selling luxury spa candles on Etsy, you'll want to do some research on the platform to find the average price for a 5.8-ounce candle in your niche. If your competition is selling their candles for an average price of $21, pricing your candle at $8.59 will seem too cheap by comparison. This will hurt your market positioning as a luxury brand and could actually result in fewer sales.

If the average price for similar candles on Etsy is $21 then you could start by charging $20. We've generally found that choosing a price that's $1–$3 cheaper than average for your niche is a great place to start.

Returning to the traditional metric of charging three to four times your cost for direct sales, a price of $20 for a candle that costs you $6.61 to make and package is charging slightly over three times the cost. This makes $20 a great price to start with on all counts.

While in this example, the initial price of $8.59 (cost + 30% markup) was low compared to the market value, sometimes it could be the other way around (i.e., the initial price is too high). In this case, you'll have to temporarily lower your markup until you can decrease your costs. It will sometimes take trial and error to find the perfect pricing. Keep adjusting your expenses until you're able to achieve a price that's three to four times the cost, while staying within the price range for your target market.

Also, keep in mind that you will need to adjust your price over time to adapt to inflation, rising costs, and the changing market. A good rule of thumb is to reevaluate your pricing every six months or so. Always keep an eye on your competitors' pricing as well.

Other Factors

- *Free shipping.* If you're offering free shipping, this per-candle variable cost will need to be factored in as well. This means you'll have to charge a bit more per candle, but as discussed in chapter 6, most customers see free shipping as a perk, even if it costs a bit more up front.

- *Platform fees.* Be sure to also take into account platform fees when evaluating your final price point. If you're selling on Etsy, you will be charged 6.5% of the listed price plus the amount paid for shipping (if applicable). There's also a payment processing fee of 3% + $0.25. There are similar fees associated with other platforms and marketplaces as well, so make sure you're aware of those. If you're selling through your own website, be aware of fees associated with payment gateways, such as Stripe or Square.

- *Profit margin.* If you'd like to increase your profit margin per candle, you'll need to lower your costs. You can often save money on materials by shopping in bulk, searching for discount codes, taking advantage of sales, or buying from a different retailer. If you have a candle supply store near you, you can potentially save a lot of money by driving there and avoiding the cost of shipping the supplies altogether. Bottom line: It's worth the time to shop around and make sure you're getting the best deal. Just remember never to sacrifice quality to save a few cents per candle—you'll lose money in the end.

- *Quantity.* In addition to single candles, you can also calculate pricing for sets or bundles (e.g., a set of four aromatherapy candles) based on the same methods used above.

CHAPTER 8

Magical Marketing

If you've followed our framework up to this point, you'll have a selection of high-quality, well-branded, and perfectly priced candles. Woo-hoo!

You're more than halfway to launching your very own profitable candle business, but there's still a crucial step we need to cover: marketing.

This is where the magic happens—where your candle business goes from dream to reality and you start making more money than you've ever imagined. Get excited!

In this chapter, we'll cover the highly effective marketing strategies that will result in massive sales for your business. This is one of the longest AND most important sections of this book.

The reality is that even with an amazing product, you won't make any sales, if no one knows your product exists. This is where our marketing strategies come in.

In the following pages, you'll learn our high-performing sales strategies that are specifically tailored to the candle industry. With this approach, you'll make sales right from launch and continue to steadily grow your income as you go.

Pre-Launch

Your pre-launch begins at least one week before you officially open for business.

The pre-launch phase has two main goals:

1. To organize and coordinate your marketing efforts, so everything's ready to go on launch day
2. To generate buzz, excitement, and hype for your new business, so you can make sales from day one

Essentially, the pre-launch is designed to ensure you have a strong start and gain quick momentum, so you can generate sales right when you open.

While the main action steps are outlined below, many of the strategies, including email marketing, social media, and more, will be discussed in greater detail later in the chapter.

Here's how to organize and coordinate your marketing efforts:

- Create social media accounts and pages for your business
- Sign up for an email marketing platform and create a landing page to start collecting email addresses
- Create a list of advertisers, influencers, bloggers, or others that could help promote your business
- Launch your business website (optional—this is not strictly needed if you're selling on a platform like Etsy or Facebook Marketplace, but still good to have)

Here's how to generate buzz, excitement, and hype for your new business:

- Tell everyone about your business and we mean EVERYONE. Your family, friends, and neighbors. People from your spin class, community group, kids' school, or social media—basically, anywhere that you find the opportunity. Don't be afraid to be loud and proud. You're starting your own business! That's a huge accomplishment and most people will be happy to support you in that.

- Hand out flyers, coupons, or samples with the exact date you'll be open for business. You can also post flyers on community bulletin boards and any other spaces designed for promotional materials (just make sure you have permission first).

- As soon as you have email set up, start gathering email addresses. You can do this through a landing page where interested customers can sign up to receive updates about your business.

- Once your social media accounts are set up, post regularly to build hype for your business. Share updates, behind-the-scenes photos, and anything else that gets your followers excited for launch day.

- Add a countdown clock to your website or email showing how many days are left until launch. We like the one from Elfsight Apps.

- Ask friends and family to share news of your launch with their people as well. This creates a ripple effect that will result in even more buzz for your business!

- Reach out to influencers, bloggers, journalists, or anyone else who can help you build buzz. Write a personalized email to each one politely asking if they would be willing to feature your launch on their website or social media account. Many micro-influencers or bloggers with 100,000 followers or less will do this in exchange for a free product.

Launch

On launch day, your business is officially open!

If you conducted the pre-launch, you should already be starting day one with visitors, customers, and sales. This is an exciting time and you need to keep the momentum going!

Here's what to do on launch day:

- *Send an email to your list letting them know your candle store is open for business.* We also suggest sending a 10% off coupon that expires in 24 hours, so you can get IMMEDIATE sales for your business.
- *Announce on all social media channels that you're officially open.* You should post multiple times throughout the day to maximize visibility. Offer a coupon or discount code here as well to drum up more sales.
- *Set up a day-one promotion.* You should announce a special promotion for launch day, such as giving the first ten customers a free gift with their purchase. This ensures quick sales and adds even more excitement to your launch!

With a well-organized launch and pre-launch, you're practically guaranteed to make sales on your very first day. After that, it's just a matter of keeping the ball rolling and increasing your sales from there.

The marketing strategies we'll discuss throughout the rest of this chapter will show you how to promote your business and grow your sales after the initial launch phase is complete.

Social Media

In this day and age, social media is an essential part of any well-rounded marketing strategy. Even if you don't use social media in your personal life, you should definitely leverage it for your business.

In this section, we'll present a list of the top social media platforms for promoting your candle business and how to make the best use of them. We recommend that you choose just TWO platforms from this list and focus your attention on those.

With social media, there's often an impulse to be everywhere at once, but trust us, when we say that it's much more effective to concentrate your efforts on the two platforms that will give you the best returns. Show up on those two platforms consistently and prioritize building an engaged audience.

Here are our recommended social media platforms for candle businesses:

Facebook

Facebook is a tried-and-true way to promote your business. Although Facebook may not be hot or new, it's still the largest social media platform with nearly 3 billion monthly users.

While there's a lot of focus on Facebook Business Pages, we highly recommend Facebook Groups because they offer better reach and allow you to communicate with your customers directly.

You can run giveaways in your Group, as well as share coupons, behind-the-scenes photos, polls, and more. The goal with Groups is to foster engagement and build relationships with customers (this leads to repeat business).

We also love Facebook ads as a low-cost way to find new leads. A lead is simply a person who is interested in your products and has the potential to become a customer.

You can run Facebook ads promoting a giveaway in your Facebook Group to gain new leads and members. For example, you can advertise a giveaway for one full-sized candle, where all new and existing members of your Group are eligible to win. This functions as an incentive for new people to join before the date of the giveaway. Just make sure you research all rules and laws pertaining to giveaways in your state or country beforehand.

Instagram

Instagram is a highly visual platform and a great way to create buzz for your business! You can share photos of your candles, quotes that relate to your niche, behind-the-scenes photos of your candle making process, and more.

While you won't necessarily make a ton of direct sales through Instagram (users tend to scroll through their feeds and rarely leave the platform), it's very effective at promoting brand awareness and getting people talking about your business. It's a great way to find your tribe and home in on your ideal customer.

If you post consistently on Instagram (once per day), you'll be able to build a following quickly and give your business a nice boost! Just be sure to use relevant hashtags to maximize visibility. You can use up to 30 hashtags per post with 3–5 being optimal. You should also use the same filter and aesthetic throughout your posts, so your account will be recognizable and uniform.

Pinterest

Pinterest is our favorite platform for direct candle sales. Although Pinterest is often considered social media, it operates more like a visual search engine.

The user types a query into the search bar and Pinterest gives them relevant Pins to look through and click on (similar to how searching on Google leads to a list of relevant sites). A Pin is basically just a visual bookmark that users can click on or save for later.

This process results in many users clicking your Pin, which leads directly to your candle business. In fact, this process is so effective that an impressive 90% of weekly users make purchase decisions on Pinterest.

In order to effectively promote your business on Pinterest, you'll need to:

- *Create a Pinterest Business Account.* This is free and comes with many useful features, such as access to analytics and the ability to run Promoted Pins (aka Pinterest Ads).

- *Create eye-catching Pins with both text and graphics.* While photos alone can work well, adding text to your Pin helps you better target your ideal customers. Also be sure that your Pins are the correct dimensions to maximize visibility in users' feeds. The current optimal size for Pins is 1000 x 1500 pixels, but check Pinterest regularly for any updates. We recommend Canva or PicMonkey for creating Pins.

- *Add relevant keywords to your Pin descriptions.* Perform keyword research on Pinterest by searching for your niche or product (e.g., spa candles) and seeing what search suggestions come up. Use the most relevant keywords in your Pin description. Just be sure that the description makes sense and you're not stuffing it with too many keywords.

- *Use a Pin scheduler like Tailwind to post your Pins throughout the day.* Once you create your Pins, you'll need to post them to Pinterest. This can be done manually, but it's much easier to use a pin scheduler, so you can post them at regular intervals resulting in more visibility.

- *Consistently share new content and create Fresh Pins.* A Fresh Pin is defined by Pinterest as images or videos that haven't been seen before. Their algorithm increasingly prioritizes Fresh Pins, so keep creating new content to boost views and clicks to your candle business.

TikTok

TikTok is the fastest-growing social media platform, especially among ages 16–34, where users share content in the form of short videos. Depending on what demographic you want to target, TikTok can be a beneficial part of your social media strategy.

You can use TikTok to post short videos of how your candles are made, tips for using your candles, quick tutorials, or simply short videos of your candles burning (you can get creative with these using filters, backgrounds, and music). Use relevant hashtags to drive traffic to your videos.

If you're comfortable with it, you can even use TikTok Live to interact with your audience in real time. You can use this to introduce new candles, host a short candle making class, announce a new product, and more.

You can also promote sales by running a TikTok challenge, where participants can share their own videos of your candles for a chance to win a prize.

Choose Your Platforms

In choosing which two social media platforms to focus on, think about your ideal customer base and where they like to hang out. Each of these platforms draws a slightly different demographic (e.g., TikTok targets a younger demographic than Facebook), so do your research and choose your social media strategy accordingly.

Regardless of which platforms you choose, it's most important to be consistent and active on them. Post regularly, respond to comments, and focus on engaging your audience. If you do this every day, the sales will follow.

Video Content

When considering your social media strategy, it's important to note that video content is increasing in popularity and generally enjoys higher visibility than photos or text posts. All of the social media platforms above allow video content, which can be a great way to boost your numbers and sales.

Focus on creating well-branded and engaging videos that speak directly to your ideal customer. Your videos don't have to be fancy (you can use your phone camera), but make sure the audio and video quality are clear. Short videos (60 seconds or less) typically convert the best, so learn to dissect your marketing message into short, bite-sized pieces for the best engagement.

Just like anything else, video is a skill and you'll get more adept with it as you practice!

Email Marketing

While social media is great for attracting new leads and creating buzz for your business, email marketing has two main purposes:

1. Nurturing new leads into customers
2. Encouraging repeat business from existing customers

You'll need an email marketing platform in order to send emails to customers. We use ConvertKit, but there are many others, such as MailChimp, MailerLite, and Constant Contact. Many of these platforms have free plans with limited features, so you can test them out first.

Lead Magnet

First things first, you'll need to incentivize leads and customers to join your email list. The best way to do this is to offer a lead magnet, such as a free gift or coupon upon sign-up.

We recommend offering a 10% or 15% off coupon as a lead magnet, but you can also offer a free digital gift that the customer can download. If you opt for a digital gift, it should be related to your niche (e.g., a store specializing in aromatherapy candles could provide a PDF of the 10 best aromatherapy scents for relaxation).

You can create a form or landing page within your email marketing platform, where people can enter their email address in exchange for the lead magnet. Once the customer signs up for your list, you'll need to deliver the lead magnet via a welcome sequence.

Welcome Sequence

Your welcome sequence is where you'll deliver your lead magnet and begin nurturing your new leads into customers (or existing customers into repeat customers). It consists of a series of emails that are automatically sent at timed intervals after someone subscribes to your list.

Here's an example of a basic welcome sequence:

Email 1 (sent immediately): Introduce yourself and your business; deliver your lead magnet

Email 2 (sent one day later): Share information about your best-selling candles (if your lead magnet is a coupon, this email will direct them toward what to buy, if they haven't made a purchase yet)

Email 3 (sent three days later): Share helpful information related to your business or niche that may encourage customers to make a purchase (the benefits of burning candles, the all-natural ingredients you use in your candles, what makes your candles different/special/better than others, etc.); remind them again to use their coupon before it expires

Throughout the sequence, be sure to emphasize how happy you are that the subscriber has joined and that they can always reply to you with any questions or feedback.

Once you decide on the content of your welcome sequence, you can set it up through your email marketing platform. Every platform has a variety of tutorials and articles that will make setup easy, even if it's your first time.

Pro tip: Make sure your welcome sequence is set up BEFORE you share forms or landing pages to ensure your subscriber receives their coupon or free gift right away.

Newsletter

In addition to the welcome sequence, we recommend a regular newsletter to keep subscribers engaged. This helps customers get to know you and continue to make purchases, even after initial sign-up.

A biweekly newsletter (sent every two weeks) typically works best, but you could choose weekly or monthly instead. Within your newsletter, you should include updates about your business, helpful candle tips, fun facts or quotes (related to your niche), and anything else that feels fun, interesting, or relevant.

Always seek to provide VALUE through your emails first and foremost. Keep your customers engaged and excited about what you have to say. This will result in higher open rates, fewer unsubscribes, and, ultimately, MORE sales.

You should also send the occasional coupon or discount to boost sales and thank subscribers for staying on your list. Your subscribers are your most loyal customers—give them the VIP treatment!

Listings

A product listing is simply the product page for each item you sell. This includes the product name, photo, description, and other relevant information.

Your product listings are, in many ways, your most important form of advertisement. This section is about how your candles are described and photographed for your Etsy shop or website.

Even if your social media and email marketing are strong, if your products are poorly described or your photos look blurry and unprofessional, you will still struggle to make sales. This section ensures this won't happen to you.

Description

Copywriting is a HUGE part of marketing. Although not all of us are natural writers, strong copywriting is a skill that can be developed with practice.

When writing descriptions for your candles, think about your ideal customer and why this candle would appeal to them. With candles, especially, it's important to be descriptive and think about how the candle will make your customer FEEL when they light it.

Don't just describe the candle objectively by saying something like, "This candle is pink and smells like roses." Go a step further with "This beautiful candle glows a soft pink with a floral scent reminiscent of a dozen long-stemmed roses."

Remember that candles aren't a necessity like food or clothing. There are two primary reasons that customers purchase candles:

1. They want to feel a certain way (such as relaxed, energized, or passionate).
2. They want to evoke the feeling of a certain place/food/memory (such as the beach, pumpkin pie, or Christmas).

The more you can home in on these feelings with your copy, the more sales you will make.

Photography

A picture is worth a thousand words. Many people buy candles to beautify their home, so gorgeous photos are a must!

Your photos should be clear, eye-catching, and professional. Make sure you show off all sides, angles, and any relevant details that will help customers make purchase decisions.

You don't need a fancy camera to take good photos. You can take beautiful photos on your phone, if you have the right lighting and backdrop.

Natural light is ideal for taking product photos or you can purchase a basic lightbox for $20–$30 on Amazon. Use editing software or an app to clean up your photos and make them pop (just don't overdo it—you want the photo to look natural and be a true representation of the product).

Also be sure that your photos are the right size and ratio for the platform. For example, on Etsy, photos should be at least 2000 pixels on the shortest side with an aspect ratio of 4:3.

If you struggle with copywriting or photography, you can also look into hiring a professional. Fiverr and Upwork have many affordable copywriters—just make sure you look at reviews and samples. In terms of photography, new or student photographers will often take photos at a reduced rate (sometimes even for free) in exchange for the opportunity to build their portfolios.

Reviews

While reviews aren't a direct part of marketing, they will help you make more sales. Think about this: If two candles have a similar scent and price, but one has 4.5 stars with 100 reviews and one has no reviews, which one are you more likely to purchase? There is a direct correlation between reviews and sales, so the more positive reviews you have, the faster your business will grow.

Reviews are essentially social proof and a key way to build trust with those who are new to your business. In fact, a 2021 report by

PowerReviews found that over 99.9% of customers read reviews when they shop online.

So, how do you get those highly coveted reviews? You ask for them! Insert a note or card in every package thanking the customer for their purchase and asking for a review. You can also ask for reviews in confirmation and follow-up emails. Be genuine and direct when asking for a review without being pushy or spammy.

A giveaway is also a great way to get those early reviews alongside building buzz for your new business. Post a giveaway on social media (if you don't have many followers yet, run a low-cost ad to direct people to the giveaway page) and then encourage the winners to post a review, once they've tried out the product. While you can't require that they leave a review, most are happy to do so—just be sure they disclose that they received the candle for free when leaving their review.

Remember that reviews are voluntary. While you can (and should) request reviews, you should NEVER pay, beg, or force someone to leave a review. You only want honest reviews from real people who have tried your products.

We also recommend sharing reviews on social media, as this can be very effective at driving sales. Yotpo Data found that when reviews are shared on social media, the conversion rate is 8.4 times higher for Twitter and 40 times higher for Facebook. You should definitely take advantage of this free marketing hack by reposting short quotes from your best reviews to social media.

Customer Loyalty

Repeat customers are a huge part of building a profitable and sustainable business. This is why effective marketing isn't just about finding new customers, but also nurturing existing ones.

As mentioned earlier, repeat customers tend to spend more on their order (67% more to be exact) than new customers because they trust you enough to purchase more expensive products and larger quantities. They're also 50% more likely to refer friends to your business and create positive word of mouth.

While you should, of course, always strive to bring new customers in, don't overlook your existing customers in the process. Encourage all customers to join your email list, Facebook Group, or follow you on social media, so you can stay in contact with them and provide incentives for repeat business.

Send out coupons, announce sales, and share fun little stories, tips, and tidbits with customers. Bring them into your world and make them feel like they're part of your inner circle with a bit of VIP treatment.

It costs five times more to acquire a new customer than it does to keep a current one, so consider customer retention at the forefront of your marketing strategy. It will pay off big time in the long run!

Other Ways to Market

Here are some other effective marketing tools for your candle business:

- *In-person or online events.* Events are a great way to spread the word and build excitement around your business. In-person events include participating in festivals, markets, craft fairs, or anywhere else that your ideal customer hangs out, while online events can include giveaways, challenges, and more.

- *Referrals.* You can incentivize both repeat AND new business by having a referral program. For example, if an existing customer refers a friend to your store and the friend makes a purchase, they both get 20% off.

- *Affiliate program.* This is similar to a referral program, but it casts a wider net. With an affiliate program, content creators (such as bloggers or influencers) place a trackable link to your shop that pays them a small commission for each sale they make (usually between 5%–30%—we recommend 10% to start). The commission is in exchange for their marketing efforts. By incentivizing others to market on your behalf, you'll reach a larger network of customers that you wouldn't have access to otherwise.

- *Word of mouth.* Telling everyone about your business doesn't end after the launch phase. You should always be spreading the word about new products or developments in your business and asking others (friends, customers, etc.) to do the same.

- *Collaborations.* Collaboration is a powerful marketing tool. This can involve forming partnerships with influencers or bloggers to promote your business. Many with smaller followings (100,000 followers or less) will often promote your business in exchange for a free product. If you want to collaborate with a larger content creator, you'll typically need to pay them, so be sure to request their media kit up front (this will include their rates, stats, etc.). You can also collaborate with another related business in a way that benefits both of you. For example, if you sell spa candles, you could partner with a local spa by giving them free candles, in exchange for advertising your store to their clients.

- *Content creation.* A great way to drive more customers to your business is by creating value-led content that's related to your niche. This could mean starting a blog, YouTube channel, or podcast. An example could be creating a meditation blog that drives readers to your meditation candle shop. If this feels like too much work, you could also guest blog or be a guest on someone else's podcast. As long as the platform reaches your ideal customer, it will be an effective way to drive sales.

- *Giveaways.* We've mentioned giveaways several times throughout this section because they're an amazing marketing tool that can achieve multiple purposes. You can use a giveaway to grow your email list or social media following, request reviews, and build general buzz for your business. When people sign up for a giveaway, you can ask them to opt into your email list, follow you on social media, join your Facebook Group, and more. Once winners are chosen, you can request that they leave a review for the product they received, if your selling platform allows this. Giveaways are super easy to set up (we recommend Rafflecopter or ViralSweep) and very effective. The only caveat is that there are local laws and guidelines pertaining to giveaways, so be sure to do your research beforehand. A notable one is "no purchase necessary," which prohibits you from requiring that users make a purchase in order to enter the giveaway.

- *Discovery or sample kits.* As we've mentioned before, it can be difficult for customers to know exactly how a candle will smell from a written description. This is why discovery or sample kits can be a great marketing tool. This is basically just a set of small 1-ounce candles in different scents that customers can purchase for a nominal fee (usually $10–$15 for six different candles). If the customer likes the samples, they will usually go on to buy one or more full-sized candles.

- *Seasonal trends and holidays.* Plan to take full advantage of seasonal trends and holidays. While you should always sell your most popular and signature candles all year round, you should also introduce limited-edition seasonal and holiday candles throughout the year. This keeps your business fresh and exciting, while also creating a sense of urgency for customers to make quick purchases before they're gone. Bath & Body Works uses this technique especially well by selling candles like Firecracker Pop and Beach Weather only during the summer and Gingerbread Marshmallow and Tree Farm only in the winter.

At this point, you have TONS of strategies and ideas for marketing your candle business. Pick the ones that work best for you and stick with them until you see results.

Remember that a high-quality product plus effective marketing ensures a highly profitable business. You're well on your way!

CHAPTER 9

Keep Growing

Now that your candles and marketing are all ready to go, what's next?

In this chapter, we'll explore the technical side of running a business, including setting up an LLC, choosing insurance, and filing taxes.

While these aspects of business can sometimes be daunting, especially to newbies, we'll break down each concept in simple terms, so it's easy to understand and effortless to apply.

Before we dive in, just a quick disclaimer that we are not lawyers, accountants, or financial experts of any kind. You should always consult a professional before making any legal or tax-related decisions for your business.

LLC

An LLC, or limited liability company, offers many benefits that will protect your business and help it grow faster.

The primary purpose of an LLC is to maintain a legal separation between your personal and business assets, but there are other benefits as well, including pass-through taxation and an Employer Identification Number (EIN).

Pass-through taxation means business income is only taxed once at the personal level, which ensures that you won't be taxed twice. An EIN will allow you to open a business bank account and apply for a resale certificate, which can give you access to tax-free wholesale prices on your candle making supplies.

Although there is a yearly fee to maintain your LLC (usually $100–$300 per year, depending on the state), the tax benefits will likely more than make up for this.

Here's the basic step-by-step process for setting up an LLC. This process can vary a bit by state, so make sure you do your own research and consult a professional whenever necessary.

1. *Choose a name for your LLC.* Make sure the name is available and fits within the naming guidelines for your state. If your LLC is a different name than your store, you will also need a "doing business as" (DBA) that is your store name (this is a simple process that just requires an additional form).
2. *Choose a resident agent in your state.* Most states require a resident agent when forming an LLC. This is a person or business entity that accepts tax and legal documents on behalf of your business.
3. *File the articles of organization with your state.* This is a simple form that you fill out and mail to the designated department within your state along with any associated fees. They are also sometimes called articles of incorporation.

That's it! The process is easier than most people think and is well worth the effort to protect your business.

Please note that the process above is for US businesses, so if you live or operate in a different country, you should research the steps to register your business there.

Licenses

In some cases, a general business license or permit may be needed to operate your candle business. Most of the time, if you're running your business from home or just online, you won't need this, but it's still a good idea to double-check, as every locale and business is different.

Some areas also require a Certificate of Occupancy (or Home Occupation Permit, if you're operating out of your home) depending on local zoning regulations. This will usually be obtained from the city or county through your local building department.

You should always check the government websites for your state, county, or city to ensure you're complying with all current requirements. If you stay on top of this, you can save yourself a lot of time and hassle later on!

Insurance

Insurance is a must for your candle business. It protects you in the event of property damage and liability claims.

This section will be general, since insurance varies greatly between countries and even states, but here are some basics you need to know:

- Check all federal, state, county, and local laws for insurance requirements. Do your research and consult with a professional, if needed.

- Shop around to find the best price and coverage for your needs. Insurance shouldn't be too costly—typically just a few hundred dollars a year when your business is small. Check your policy and make sure you're only paying for what you need (and nothing you don't).

- Types of insurance:
  - *General liability* – this is typically the minimum policy that is required; it covers a broad range of risks, including bodily injury, property damage, medical payments, and more.
  - *Product liability* – this is highly recommended for candle businesses; it provides protection in the event that a customer or their property is harmed by your product.
  - *Workers' compensation* – this is usually only needed if you have employees; it provides financial support to employees who are unable to work because of job-related injury or sickness.

- There are other types of policies that cover a wide range of risks, including crafters insurance, home-based business insurance, and small business insurance. Do your research and choose accordingly.

Taxes

While tax season is never fun, you can make the process much easier on yourself by staying organized and tracking your expenses throughout the year. Many small businesses need to file estimated quarterly taxes, so staying on top of your taxes all year is the smart thing to do.

In order to stay organized, we highly recommend opening a business bank account and applying for a business credit card. This will make it infinitely easier to track your expenses, income, and profits. Keep your personal and business assets separate to avoid a giant headache later on.

In addition, we like to keep track of our expenses and profits in an Excel sheet. Every time we purchase something for our business, whether it's an item or a service, we record it in the Excel sheet and then track our profits there too. You can also use accounting software like QuickBooks.

To file your taxes, we recommend hiring an accountant (this is often less of an expense than you would think, especially when your business is small) or using tax software, such as TurboTax or H&R Block. Both of these have an easy and cost-effective option where you can file taxes yourself, but with access to expert help, so you can ask questions along the way.

That's it! We kept this chapter short and sweet since every business is different when it comes to insurance, accounting, and taxes.

Our main purpose here is to steer you in the right direction and show you that the technical side of running a business isn't so scary. Honestly, the hardest part is simply getting started.

There are plenty of resources out there to help, so always do your research, ask questions, and don't be afraid to just dive in! You'll be glad you did and your business will thrive because of it.

CHAPTER 10

Make Money on Autopilot

Congrats! You've made it to our final and favorite chapter. Here, we'll teach you the magic of passive income and how to make money with your business while you sleep, vacation, spend time with family, and more.

Passive income is essentially money that you earn without active work. Very often it means putting in the work up front and then continuing to collect income over time (e.g., writing and publishing a book once and then collecting royalties even decades later). Instead of directly trading your time for dollars, you can set up your candle business to work FOR you with minimal time and effort on your part.

This chapter is what really sets our book apart from other candle business books. Most people think that a candle business is hands-on and it usually is. After all, you have to make the candles, set up shop, do the marketing—none of this sounds particularly passive, right?

We're here to flip the script and show you the exact strategies you'll need to take your business to a level where your day-to-day presence isn't required and money flows into your bank account automatically.

The amazing thing about starting your own candle business is that it can be as hands-on or hands-off as you want it to be! You get to choose how involved you want to be in your own business. At the beginning, it will inevitably be more hands-on, but eventually, over time you can build it to the point where it's almost entirely passive.

Ready for this? We're so excited!

Work Flow

While this first strategy isn't totally passive, it will result in greater efficiency and, ultimately, less work.

Work flow, in this context, is simply about creating a streamlined system for your business. The goal is to always know what you need to do next, so you can move quickly between tasks.

Here's an example of an efficient work flow for fulfilling customer orders:

1. Print shipping labels
2. Tape shipping labels to boxes
3. Package each candle in the correct box
4. Tape all boxes closed
5. Drop them at the shipping location

Plan to complete this process just once at the end of the workday, instead of each time a customer places an order. If you package and ship all the orders at once, it will be much faster and result in less distraction throughout the day.

In this day and age, the eight-hour or more workday is becoming largely unnecessary for most desk jobs. Research has found that a forced nine-to-five schedule often causes people to fill time with needless busy work and redundant tasks.

To combat this, choose to run your business in a task-oriented way instead of based on time. Each day, make a list of tasks you need to complete and cross each one off as you go. You should measure productivity in the tasks you complete instead of the number of hours worked. When you finish your task list for the day (even if it's only been four hours), you're done with work. Rest up, so you can have another efficient workday tomorrow.

By streamlining your day and eliminating unnecessary tasks, you'll find that you're able to complete more work in less time. If you focus on the right tasks (the ones that will move your business forward the most), this will inevitably result in MORE income per hour worked.

In doing this, you'll begin putting an end to the mentality of trading time for money, which will set you up for passive income later on.

Outsource

Outsourcing is one of the best ways to make your business passive. It simply involves hiring out the tasks you would normally do yourself and taking a hands-off approach to your business.

Outsourcing also makes sense in terms of efficiency. If a specific task takes you five hours to complete, why not hire a professional who can complete it in three hours? If another task frustrates you, why not hire a professional who actually enjoys it?

Here are examples of tasks that you can outsource:

- *Candle making* – This is a time-consuming and obvious task to hire out, unless you really enjoy making the candles yourself. A cost-effective way to outsource this task is to a hire an "apprentice" or trainee, who is willing to work alongside you for modest pay in exchange for learning the ropes. Over time, the trainee can take over the task completely for an increase in pay. A great place to start is to reach out to local art schools and see if any of the students would be interested in working with you. You can also purchase candles wholesale, instead of making them yourself, which we'll discuss in the next section.

- *Shipping and fulfillment* – As business picks up, you'll find yourself spending more time fulfilling and shipping orders. This is when you'll want to consider hiring out this task by posting the job on Indeed or Upwork. You can also consider dropshipping, if you purchase your candles wholesale, which we'll discuss later.

- *Photography* – Unless you're a professional photographer, this is a great task to hire out early, so you can experience a boost in the quality of your photos (which will also result in more sales). A cost-effective way to do this is to hire a student or up-and-coming freelance photographer, who is willing to work for reduced rates (or sometimes even for free) in exchange for a reference and the opportunity to build their portfolio.

- *Social media/email/general marketing* – There are tons of freelance marketers out there, who specialize in social media management, email marketing, publicity, and so much more. In addition to making your business more hands-off, a strong online marketer can significantly increase your sales! You can find many qualified freelancers on Upwork or similar sites— just be sure to check their references and conduct thorough interviews to find the best ones for your business. Oftentimes, one very well-qualified candidate can take care of ALL your marketing needs (as opposed to hiring multiple people).

- *General tasks* – A good assistant can free up your time by taking a multitude of tasks off your plate. If your business is entirely online, you can save money by hiring a virtual assistant, which is an independent contractor who works remotely.

- *Management* – If you want your business to be completely hands-off, you'll need to hire someone to manage day-to-day operations for you. This is generally the last step to making your business totally passive. Be sure to conduct a thorough hiring process and make sure this is someone with experience who you can trust.

It's important to note that you probably won't need to hire a separate person for each of the areas above. Oftentimes, one employee can be charged with multiple tasks. For example, the person you hire for candle making could also handle shipping and fulfillment.

Depending on the size and scope of your business, it will likely only take 2–4 employees to outsource it completely. Many of these jobs can be hired out to contractors or freelancers as well.

As you've probably guessed by now, the only real downside to outsourcing is that it requires capital to hire employees and contractors—typically, more capital than you'll have at the beginning stages of your business.

If outsourcing is your goal, you'll need to be patient. In general, you'll need to do the work yourself at the beginning to save money and learn the ropes of the business.

Once your business is stable and profitable, you can begin hiring out tasks one by one. Start by hiring out your most difficult, time-consuming, or least favorite task first and keep going from there. With each person you hire, your workload will be easier and you'll gain more time back.

Eventually, your business will be completely passive. It takes some time and tenacity, but it's worth it in the end to have a thriving business that deposits money in your account every month with minimal work on your part.

Keep in mind that outsourcing isn't just a path to passive income, but also a way to increase sales and, ultimately, profits. If you're outsourcing correctly, you should be hiring experts who can complete a task as well or, oftentimes, better than you can, resulting in an overall revenue increase for your business. It's a win-win!

Make sure you're also aware of local laws, guidelines, insurance, and anything else pertaining to hiring employees. It's generally easier to hire contractors or freelancers to start. Most of the roles in your business won't necessarily require a full-time employee.

Finally, be sure to always treat your employees and contractors well and fairly, just like you would your most loyal customers. When those working for you feel happy, respected, and heard, they will become your greatest asset and your business will thrive.

Wholesale

If you've followed our book up to this point, you will be both the supplier and the retailer for your business. This means that you make the candles AND you sell them.

However, if you purchase already-made candles from wholesale suppliers instead, you'll cut a whole step out of the process and become JUST the retailer. This alone can cut your workload in half.

With this strategy, you'll purchase candles from wholesale suppliers and then sell them through your store. This can be a bit more costly than making them yourself, but much easier.

Choosing a Supplier

To start, you can find a candle wholesale supplier by checking candle companies that you already know and love to see if they do wholesale orders.

To see an example, check out the wholesale page from Scented Designs (this is a soy candle company that we absolutely love) by going to scenteddesigns.com/pages/wholesale-candles. This will give you an idea of what to expect when you're ordering wholesale.

Be sure to do your research and choose a wholesale supplier that aligns with your niche, ideal customer base, and values. For example, if your niche is natural candles with a clean burn then you should find a wholesale supplier that offers exactly that.

Just like when making your own candles, always consider your ideal customer and what would appeal to them, first and foremost. If you don't choose a wholesale supplier that matches the expectations of your customers, you will not make sales—period.

Many wholesale suppliers offer sample sets for purchase, so you can make sure their candles are in line with your expectations. We highly recommend taking advantage of this, so you know exactly what you're getting before placing a bulk order.

In summary, choose your wholesale suppliers carefully, as the quality of their candles reflects on your business. Cutting corners on this could lead to losing customers, so it's essential to prioritize their satisfaction.

Selling Wholesale Candles

There are two primary ways to sell wholesale candles. The first is to have the candles delivered directly to you, so you can stock, fulfill, and ship the orders yourself.

Once you've chosen a supplier, you can start by ordering 25–50 candles in two to three different scents or styles. This is a relatively small order, so you can determine what's popular with your customers before ordering more. You may need to experiment with different suppliers to figure out what works best for your business. Once you find one or more suppliers that you love, the rest is easy—just rinse and repeat!

When pricing your candles, you can still follow the process from chapter 7, but use the wholesale purchase price per candle instead of the raw ingredients when calculating variable cost. You should still take into account any shipping, packaging, and fixed costs.

Overall, this first option gives you more control over your business, but is also more hands-on than the option we'll discuss next.

The second option for selling wholesale candles is dropshipping. Dropshipping is an order fulfillment process in which your business doesn't actually stock the products it sells. Instead, the retailer (that's you) purchases inventory from a wholesaler as needed to fulfill orders.

Basically, instead of holding stock yourself, you'll rely on a third party to handle inventory and order fulfillment. This option is almost entirely passive and, in many ways, lower risk, since you don't have to purchase the inventory up front. On the flip side, your profits will likely be lower (on average, 20%–30% profit per sale) than if you fulfilled the orders yourself.

Typically with dropshipping, you will choose a supplier, set your own price, and then sell their candles through your website, Etsy shop, or other selling platform. When orders come through, they will automatically be sent to the supplier, who will then fulfill and ship the orders.

As a quick Google search will show, there are many dropship candle suppliers out there. We really like Wax & Wick for soy candles, as they offer discounts for higher sale volumes. You can find a full list of dropship candle suppliers here: nichedropshipping.com/dropship-candles.

If you choose to use dropshipping, the process of supplying, fulfilling, and shipping the candles will be completely passive. This will decrease your active workload significantly and you'll primarily be left with marketing and management tasks. If you hire those out as well, say hello to a passive business!

Digital Products

Imagine creating an item just once and being able to sell it a thousand times over without any additional work. This is the magic of digital products.

Digital products are at the core of the passive income revolution. We strongly feel that every e-commerce business should have at least a few digital products that complement their physical products.

So, first off, what is a digital product? It's simply an item that exists in digital form. Instead of receiving a physical item that is shipped to them, a customer who purchases a digital item will download it straight to their computer, smartphone, or other device.

This means instant access for the customer and NO active fulfillment on your part. With digital items, you put the work in once by creating the product and putting it up for sale. After that, the product sells indefinitely without any additional work on your part. The result is automated passive income.

Your digital product should relate to your niche, appeal to your ideal customer, or complement your candles in some way. The ideal digital product will meet all three of these goals.

We recommend creating and selling printables to start. They're quick, easy, and customers love them! They're especially popular on Etsy.

A printable is simply a digital product that the customer can download and then print, such as checklists, PDFs, or worksheets. You can create a printable in just a few hours using a graphic design platform like Canva or PicMonkey. Both of these platforms have templates and tutorials that will show you how.

As an example, if you sell meditation candles, you could create and sell meditation coloring pages in your shop as well. Other ideas include a reference sheet showing the benefits and uses of common essential oils or a PDF that shows how to choose the best candle for each room in your house. It all depends on your niche. The more closely you relate your printable to your niche, the more passive income you will make.

You can sell a single one-page printable or a pack of printables. A single printable will generally be priced between $0.99 and $1.99, while a pack of printables can range from $2.99 to $19.99 or more depending on how many pages it has.

Another option is to create an online candle making course or another type of course related to your niche (e.g., a course on how to blend essential oils). This can be a series of shorter classes with an hour or so of content, or a larger course with several hours of content.

A shorter class should succinctly but completely cover one specific topic. An example of this would be a one-hour video class on how to choose the right wax for your candle.

The alternative is a well-formatted, multi-hour video course with PDFs, checklists, and worksheets to help the student really absorb the material.

This is more work up front, but courses like this can sell for up to $100 and sometimes more.

We recommend Teachable or Thinkific for creating online courses. Both platforms have a free plan you can start with.

To make a video course, start by brainstorming your content and breaking it up into lessons. Think about all the information a student would need to know in order to master the topic. After that, write down your talking points and film yourself presenting and demonstrating the lessons. You can film the videos easily using your phone or computer— it doesn't need to be fancy, as long as the information is there. After you're done creating the videos, you can add other materials (such as checklists or worksheets) wherever you feel they would be most helpful.

If a course feels like too much, you could also consider delivering the same information in another format, such as an e-book.

Regardless of which digital products you choose, our best advice is to know your customer base. If you choose a digital product that your ideal customer really wants, you will make nearly instant passive income.

We hope this chapter got you excited for the possibility of passive income! While the strategies here are totally optional, the more you automate your business, the more free time you'll have for the other things that matter to you in life.

Work-life balance is SO important and we encourage you to explore these options when you're ready. As we mentioned before, your business can be as active or passive as you'd like it to be. You can choose to implement all of these strategies or just some—do what works best for you!

Finally, keep in mind that all passive income streams require either time or capital before they can become truly passive. Even with the most passive types of income, such as dividend or portfolio income (aka investing in stocks), you'll need to make the money first in order to grow your portfolio. Nothing comes entirely for free, but it's all worth it in the long run.

Your business needs to be stable and profitable before it can be passive. Like in our earlier example, it may take a year to write and market a book, but once it's selling consistently, you could make passive income for decades to come.

Who knows? In a year or two, you could be sipping a piña colada on the beach in Hawaii, while your candle business makes six figures on autopilot. If this is your goal, you have all the strategies you need right here. Just keep going and don't give up!

Cheat Sheet:
Launch Your Business in 30 Days

Before we end, we'd like to offer you a FREE bonus cheat sheet as a thank you for reading our book!

This short PDF guide contains our simple step-by-step framework for launching your candle business in just 30 days. It streamlines the process described in this book, so you can open your business quickly and make money faster!

Just sign up at boundlessbooks.ck.page/candle and we'll deliver the cheat sheet straight to your inbox!

Let's Do It!

Congrats! You've made it to the end and are ready to build your candle empire.

Just a few quick words of advice before you go:

1. *Take action.* Your six-figure candle business only starts when YOU take action. Although this book has all the steps and guidance you need to be successful, simply reading it isn't enough. Don't stall—get started today and you'll already be one step closer to achieving your dreams!

2. *Be consistent.* Building your candle business is as simple as showing up every day. Even if you can't commit to it full-time yet, we still encourage you to dedicate at least some time to your business on a daily basis. Even an hour a day will move you forward. One of our favorite quotes: "Little by little, a little becomes a lot."

3. *Don't give up.* Just like anything else, you'll have days when your candle business lights up your life and other days where it feels a bit more difficult. No matter what—don't give up! Enjoy the good days and keep working through the hard ones. It's worth it and you'll get there.

We wish you all the success in the world. Thanks for being here and good luck!

If you found this book helpful, could you please leave a quick review or rating on Amazon? This means the world to us and helps the right readers find our book!

Resources

Adamson, C. (2021). "Palm Wax 101: Palm Wax for Candle Making." Retrieved from https://www.candleers.com/palm-wax-101-palm-wax-for-candle-making/.

Bouhl, G. (2023). "What Licenses Does A Candle Making Business Need?" Retrieved from https://startingyourbusiness.com/what-licenses-does-a-candle-making-business-need/.

CandleScience. (2022). "How to Price Your Candles." Retrieved from https://www.candlescience.com/how-to-price-your-candles/.

Clark, J. (2023). "18 Online Review Statistics Every Marketer Should Know." Retrieved from https://www.searchenginejournal.com/online-review-statistics/329701/.

Connolly, B. (2023). "How to Sell on Facebook Marketplace – 2023 Beginner's Guide." Retrieved from https://www.junglescout.com/blog/how-to-sell-on-facebook-marketplace/.

Doyle, B. (2023). "TikTok Statistics." Retrieved from https://wallaroomedia.com/blog/social-media/tiktok-statistics/.

Federal Trade Commission. (2023). "Fair Packaging and Labeling Act: Regulations Under Section 4 of the Fair Packaging and Labeling Act." Retrieved from https://www.ftc.gov/legal-library/browse/rules/fair-packaging-labeling-act-regulations-under-section-4-fair-packaging-labeling-act.

Heaslip, E. (2019). "Considering Opening a Retail Store? The Pros and Cons of Brick-and-Mortar Locations." Retrieved from https://www.uschamber.com/co/start/startup/opening-brick-and-mortar-location-for-your-business.

National Candle Association. (2023). "Elements of a Candle: Wicks." Retrieved from https://candles.org/elements-of-a-candle/wicks/.

National Candle Association. (2023). "Understanding the Label." Retrieved from https://candles.org/fire-safety-candles/read-the-label/.

Nethercott, R. (2022). "5 Reasons Why Repeat Customers Are Better Than New Customers." Retrieved from https://www.constantcontact.com/blog/repeat-customers/.

O'Toole, T. (2023). "How to Start a Candle Business: A Comprehensive Guide." Retrieved from https://www.tailorbrands.com/blog/start-a-candle-business.

Pack Leader USA. (2022). "What Needs to be Included on Your Candle Label?" Retrieved from https://www.packleaderusa.com/blog/what-needs-to-be-included-on-your-candle-label.

Tank, A. (2023). "Why Working 9 to 5 Is Not Ideal For Efficient Work Today." Retrieved from https://www.lifehack.org/articles/productivity/why-9-5-joke-and-how-deal.html.

TRUiC Team. (2023). "Candle Making Insurance." Retrieved from https://howtostartanllc.com/business-insurance/business-insurance-for-candle-makers.

Other Titles by Alyssa and Garrett Garner

Etsy Business Launch: The Ultimate Guide to Making Six Figures Selling on Etsy.

About the Authors

Alyssa and Garrett are married entrepreneurs with almost a decade of experience in the online business space. They've dabbled in everything from blogging and e-commerce to publishing and real estate.

Over the years, they've discovered a practical and reproducible framework for building highly profitable businesses in a short amount of time. Now, their passion lies in teaching budding entrepreneurs how to escape the grind and find financial freedom doing what they love.

When they're not building their entrepreneurial empire, Alyssa and Garrett enjoy travel, ballroom dancing, and Broadway shows.

Thanks for reading!

Made in the USA
Las Vegas, NV
18 February 2024

85934552R00070